Angels and the Power of Prayer
Part 1 - Table of Contents

Angels and the Power of Prayer
Part 2 - Table of Contents

Angels and the Power of Prayer
Part 3 - Table of Contents

FORWARD

This account commenced quite some time ago with a collection of personal encounters with God's beautiful angels and "not so good" fallen angels, as well as those experiences of prayers heard and answered.

Many friends have asked me more than once to share by writing these true stories. After prayer and reflection, I decided to write down some of these experiences to demonstrate: 1) God's power and concern for His children; 2) that the good angels constantly watch over, protect, guide and pray for us, especially if we ask for their help; 3) that God can use even weak human beings to show His providential care.

As I shared these true accounts, my friends were more and more spontaneous about their encounters and experiences with angels and the power of prayer in their lives. As the sharings, encounters, and experiences accumulated I thought that these would encourage, strengthen and revitalize the listener or reader's faith and trust in God and His family.

As I began in earnest to pursue this important subject,

I was amazed and pleased at all the instances of God's use of His angels, and the tremendous effects of prayer recorded on practically every other page in scripture, and the lives of the Saints. They are also mentioned in the formal pronouncements of the official magisterium of the Church.

From Genesis, with the angel sent by God to guard the entrance of the garden, to the angels speaking with Abraham, Lot, Jacob, the Tobit family, Peter, and Jesus himself, as well as many others, these angels take on many shapes and forms as the events warrant. (e.g. Hebrews 13:2—"Do not be afraid to welcome strangers in your home, for some thereby have entertained angels unawares.")

As we combine meditations about the angels in the Old and New Testaments with those angelic visitations of our own day and age, we cannot help coming to the conclusion that angels deserve our awareness and acknowledgment.

ALL YE ANGELIC HOSTS, PRAISE THE LORD!

EARLY REALIZATION

I became aware of angels, God's friends, thanks to my mother's loving guidance. Besides her teaching on the subject and her wonderful example of being like Mary, she knew the power of pictures. She put up a beautiful picture of a guardian angel protecting and guiding two children across a rickety old bridge. It made a big impression on me. And, of course, I was taught the meaningful daily prayer to one's angel. "Angel of God, my guardian dear, to whom God's love commits me here, ever this day be at my side, to light, to guard, to rule and guide. Amen."

My first recollection of angelic protection over my family was when my Dad was cutting some trees on our ranch. He had stopped to get some rest under a huge shady maple tree and unexpectedly his angel told him to move over. Dad heeded the warning. Suddenly a two or three inch width of a dead maple limb came shooting straight down from the top of the tree where it had been snagged, dangling for some time. It became embedded in the ground only inches from where he was standing. If he had remained where he was the limb might have killed him.

The angels were kept busy everyday keeping track of a tomboy like me. One day, when six years old, I decided to run the full length of one of the poultry buildings on the family ranch. Thousands of birds tried desperately to fly out of my way as I ran through them. Feathers flew! I ran the full length of the building so fast that at the far end, I opened the door, went through and slammed it shut behind me. Suddenly, glancing down, I found myself perched on a narrow ledge on the second floor of the building. This would be quite a jump for an adult, but for a six year old child, it was dangerous. Looking down, I saw that my father had parked an old manure spreader underneath the ledge. I stared at the row of spikes at the end of the spreader and saw a steel bar in front of the spikes. Since I was an "exceptionally" brave child as well as an agile one, I figured I could land on the bar and not on the spikes. After landing on the bar, I felt really pleased with my athletic prowess. My plan was to walk carefully on the narrow bar to the end of the spreader and jump off. Suddenly I lost my balance, and fell on the row of sharp, dagger-like spikes, which rolled with me as I plunged down to the ground. Fortunately the machine had been left in neutral, which allowed the spikes to flow with my body weight rather than impaling me as they would have had they been locked in place.

After the injury, my spine steadily disintegrated. Two discs went almost to nothing, with calcification of the vertebrae from the neck to the coccyx, the spine becoming an "S," and one leg becoming an inch shorter due to poor circulation. There were almost always pain and aches. At night the jabbing pains would be so violent that I thought that one of the giants of fairy tale lore had pierced my back with a spear. I would cry with the pain. Thank God that Mom and Dad were so patient.

Our family Doctor fitted me out with a back brace, which helped out a lot, even getting me out of Physical Education classes in high school. Thank goodness, too, because if I ever had one of those athletic 5'10" girls hit me from the back while we were playing basketball, I would have been a "groaning goner."

In 1949, the Provincial Leader and her council accepted me, "mess and all" into the religious congregation. I was so happy to be received, in spite of being partially deaf and disabled. With this "top secret," (none of the other sisters were aware of my physical situation, though my own group of four probably wondered why I knelt down on the floor to make the beds) I went through the Novitiate.

Teaching the children, teenagers and sisters was a real source of joy for me for many years. Even though directing choirs, working with drill teams, art and science fairs caused many an ache, it was all made worthwhile; especially after reading the Fatima story of the Blessed Virgin Mary encouraging the three children to make sacrifices and accept the crosses and trials "for souls" in great need of grace and conversion. Looking at the negatives (sufferings) and changing them to positives (bringing people closer to Jesus) was worth it all.

All those years of serving with "the secret" would change dramatically in the summer of 1974, my 25th Silver Anniversary Jubilee year as a sister.

Sister Mary Frances can tell what happened next:

"Since the two of us were getting caught up in the healing ministry by this time, I prayed to God to heal my friend's back. I asked if I could, for her Jubilee gift, lay hands on her in healing prayer, as Jesus did for the sick and the children. In my head came the clear words: 'No, just pray generally for her. I have surprises too.' So I prayed generally and off she went to her retreat in Mankato, Minnesota with the School Sisters of Notre Dame."

At the end of the eight day retreat, Monsignor Rosage and his healing ministry team, which included my friend, Sister Frances Clare, S. S. N. D., all prayed with and for each person individually. Each of us in turn was asked the same question. "What do you want Jesus to do for you?" That takes the attention away from us creatures and places it on Jesus, our Savior, who is the only one that can do the healing.

After a beautiful prayer for healing in the name of Jesus, I went to the back of the chapel, knelt and silently prayed for the others who were to be prayed for. I didn't feel anything different, except for a peace that prevailed. I repeated over and over the motto on my profession ring, "Fiat Voluntas Tua," "Thy Will be done." Whatever You think is best, Lord.

That night, I awoke from a deep sleep more than once noticing something was happening to me. Not Knowing quite what it was, I turned over and was out like a light, once again.

The next morning in utter amazement and joy I awoke with absolutely no pain or aches. I felt my spine. The hump and "S" were gone. It was nice and straight. I jumped out of bed and walked across the floor with my bare feet. My legs were the same length! I wouldn't have to have the inch-thick sole on one of my shoes anymore! Thank God!

After arriving back home, I had X-rays taken of the back. It was wonderful! It looked like another person's spine picture. All the calcification between the vertebrae was gone. The two discs that had almost disappeared were nice and fat. The spine was beautifully straight. Ever since that day, every time I bend over to pick up suitcases or loads of any kind, I thank the Lord God most profusely. What a wonderful 25th anniversary He gave to His "child." I am so grateful!

HORSES! HORSES!

At eight years of age, my angels interceded to help me. My parents had taken my brother George and me to Bridge Rivers, British Columbia, Canada, to visit our grandparents. My father set up a large tent near the main house, which was at the base of a large, steep hill.

One beautiful sunny morning, I took my little brother and my three cousins to explore a narrow winding path up the steep hill. The trail had many scrub trees and rocky boulders along the path. As we five young children proceeded slowly up the hill, we could hear the "sky" begin to rumble. The sounds grew louder and louder. Even the ground was shaking and trembling. A beautiful angelic voice told me to stop, gather the children and take shelter behind a three foot boulder that was ahead of us beside the path. We all crouched down behind the large rock. Suddenly, thirty or more wild horses came racing down the trail just where we had been standing several seconds before. Even though some of the horses jumped over the boulder where we were hidden, we were safe, although very frightened. As we stood up to watch the stampede continue down the hill, I saw my mother come out of the tent, yelling our names, as the horses ran past her to the lake. A couple of them almost ran right into the tent.

As we moved from behind the rock, I noticed that we had shared this safe shelter with a colony of ants. If there had been a choice beforehand, I still would have chosen the little creatures over the horses.

WHAT ABOUT ANGELS? DO THEY EXIST?

Do Angels exist? Good and bad? I say definitely, yes. Scripture often mentions them. In Hebrew the word Malak, means "messenger." Heavenly spirits are very much in evidence from Genesis on. (Genesis 3:24,16:7ff). Abraham is prevented by the angel from sacrificing Isaac. (Genesis 22:11) Jacob was shown a vision of angels. (Genesis 28:10ff). The Angel of Yahweh came between Pharaoh's army and Moses' people and protected and guided them. (Exodus 14:19f). There are many more instances in the Old Testament.

In the New Testament we have many examples of angels. The infancy gospels: The angel warned Joseph. (Matthew 1:20). Joseph was told by an angel that it was safe to return to Bethlehem. (Matthew 2:19). The angel Gabriel announced to Mary that she was selected to be the mother of the Messiah (Luke 1:26) and gave a message to Zachariah about his son John. (Luke 1:11). The angels ministered to Jesus after His temptations, (Matthew 4:11) and during Jesus' agony, (Luke 22:43). Jesus referred to the guardian angels of little ones, (Matthew 18:10). He also said that He could summon the angels to rescue Him from His captors. (Matthew 26:43). Some of the angels fell. Jesus mentioned this when He said, "I saw Satan fall from heaven." (Luke 10:18). An explicit reference to the story of the fall of some of the angels can be found in Apocalypse 12:9-10.

A PARTING GIFT

My family had a real life experience with what appeared to be God's enemy. Just before I entered religious life, the Lord gave my family a wonderful gift: my father's baptism. My family had prayed faithfully for more than twenty years for Dad, and finally in 1948 he was now to be baptized at a small, old mission church nearby.

The morning of the baptism began quite normally. Everyone was getting dressed when the house suddenly filled with smoke. It had a strange odor, similar to sulfur or burning wire. Since our original family home had burnt down some years before, we knew we had to search every inch of the house to find the source of the smell and smoke. The entire family searched the closets, the attic, and every part of the house. We even looked under the house, but to no avail. There was no fire, but the odor was very strong.

As the time came to leave for the church, we were still

searching for the source of the problem odor. Finally, we knew if we did not leave, my father's baptism would have to be postponed to another day. Everyone agreed that it didn't matter if our house burned, Dad's baptism was worth the risk.

After the ceremony we rushed home to see if we had a house. The house was just fine. We gingerly went inside and double checked every nook and cranny. There was no trace of the horrible sulfur odor or the smoke that had engulfed the house earlier that morning. Had it been a parting obstacle from the evil one?

ANGELS AND THE CAR FIRE

Before I entered religious life, while at the university, I enjoyed being a violinist in the City Civic Symphony Orchestra. One evening, as a friend drove me to the concert, the car engine caught on fire. The wires under the hood were in flames and the flames were close to my feet. I envisioned my very flammable, formal dress exploding into flames. I quickly jumped out of the car, thinking that since the fire was in the engine and the electrical system, the car would be coming to a stop. I was wrong. We had been traveling at a high rate of speed and the vehicle had not slowed down as quickly as I anticipated. As I fell out of the car, I hit the side of the road with my toes and flew forward toward the gravel, glass and road debris. Instantly I felt something lift me gently and put me back on my feet. If I had slid into all that debris, I would have seriously injured my hands. This would have been devastating for a musician.

Several hundred yards down the road the car stopped. My friend jumped out of the car and ran back to see how badly injured I was. Miraculously, there were no cuts or bruises. The car fire went out. Opening up the hood of the car, the driver reconnected several wires, and with that the car started right up and we drove to the music hall where I played the violin for the evening's concert. This was my first actual physical encounter, as I believe, with my guardian angel.

ANGELS AND TEMPTATION

Do our guardian angels help and warn us when there is a spiritual danger?

While attending the university, on a particular evening I was on a date with a friend. We were sitting in his car talking, when my friend became too amorous. Suddenly there was a bright flash of light. My guardian angel, I believe, warned me to get away, so I jumped out of the car and raced to the house. I thanked God for guarding my virginity which was already consecrated to the Sacred Heart, and for sending my guardian angel to remind me of my promise to God.

NOVITIATE ANGELS

As a young postulant and later as a novice, I treasured all those wonderful spiritual books. After reading Tanquarey's, "The Spiritual Life," autobiographies by Sister Mary of the Trinity and Sister Elizabeth of the Trinity, I was deeply impressed and moved by the holiness, power, and giftedness of the Blessed Trinity. While in chapel one day, I prayed and then consecrated myself to the Blessed Trinity: Father, Son, and Holy Spirit. I experienced the inundation of warmth, love, peace, a fullness of awareness of the Trinity's presence in my heart and soul. I knew I was divinely occupied.

After many months of being on "cloud nine," I had to tell someone about my experience. I shared it with my novice mistress and related the whole experience to her. Her response was mystifying. She said, with a smile, "Oh, Sister, you will get over it."

Happily I have never gotten over it!

Why do I relate this personal "Baptism of the Spirit?" I share this because with almost every major grace-moment often there follows a battle and encounter with what I have discerned to be evil angels who hate God and all the good that is being accomplished.

Along with many new novices, I had been given the privilege of retiring a whole hour early in the evening. Being surrounded by four white sheets acting as curtains, I laid my head down on my pillow. Suddenly I was aware of something very evil at the foot of my bed. I stared at a very dark form which quickly attacked and tried to strangle me, at which I cried internally (I didn't want to disturb the other five sisters in the dorm.)

"Jesus, help me," were the only words I could pray.

The dark evil form let go and disappeared. Looking back on this incident, the experience of receiving special graces was a powerful source of joy and jubilation. But this experience helped me learn to be humble and trust in Jesus more, and for me to expect trials and not to be afraid of any evil, since God is infinitely more powerful. "At the name of Jesus every knee should bend, in heaven and on earth and under the earth" (Philippians 2:10).

After the pronouncement of first vows, my first teaching assignment was at brand new St. Rose Catholic Parochial Grade School in southern Washington. Being a beginning teacher I still was "contaminated" by university level vocabulary.

One day just before a big rain storm, my third grade children were unusually restless and squirming in their desks during what I thought was an interesting true story. Finally, I stopped and asked one of my best "little angels," "What are you supposed to be doing while I am teaching?"

He replied most sincerely, "Sister, we are supposed to listen to you, even if we don't understand what you are saying."

That was a good lesson for me to simplify my vocabulary to suit my third graders.

Later that week the children came filing into the classroom and amazingly enough they continued to play, shuffle and push each other. They ignored my silent signal of folding my hands in a prayerful attitude facing the students. I turned inwardly and in my spirit spoke directly to my guardian angel and to the angels guarding all my children. "Please, dear angels, remind your charges to turn around, stop what they are doing, fold their hands and be ready to pray."

To my amazement and joy, every single student stopped their various antics, immediately folded their hands, eyes downcast and ready for prayer. I heaved a grateful sigh of relief and thanked my angels for all the help.

HIGHWAY TRAGEDY AVERTED

Several months after I took my final vows, I was asked to drive five sisters to the airport in Vancouver, British Columbia. After we said "Bon voyage," to a couple of them, the other sisters and I got ready to return to Seattle (a three hour trip of one hundred sixty miles). It was late evening and the sky was jet black. The sisters and I climbed into our order's old Buick and began our usual "car prayers." I drove seventy miles an hour and felt confident that the automobile would run. After we crossed into the United States and headed south on Interstate 5, we continued on the two lane highway at that same speed. There was a large median between the southbound and northbound lanes on I-5. I passed a car and since there were so few cars, saw no reason to go back into the slow lane. Quite unexpectedly, I heard my guardian angel tell me in a calm but firm voice, "Move over." I didn't hear him audibly, but he spoke to my spirit. The words were so very clear, "Move over!" I immediately moved the car from the passing, speed lane to the outside, slower lane. As soon as I was safely in the outside lane, out of the black night came a car without headlights, speeding north at eighty miles per hour in the southbound passing lane. If we had remained in that lane one second longer, there would have been absolutely nothing left of the cars or us, since there would have been a 150 mile-an-hour impact. Again, I thanked my beautiful, invisible friend.

ALASKAN DOG

Can angels, even though they are pure spirits, take on any appearance or form they wish to, with God's power and permission? An account of St. Don Bosco is a perfect example of an angel taking on any shape needed at the time.

One particular evening Don Bosco was walking home after visiting one of his congregation when suddenly, what looked like a street person jumped out with a knife and tried to thrust it into Fr. Bosco. Just at that precise moment a very large dog leaped out of the shadows, grabbed the would-be killer's wrist and wrestled him and his knife to the ground. The dog rescued the priest from being killed. On another occasion the angel took on the appearance of a very large "guard" to accompany the saint on the way home. This "guard" saved him from being robbed.

This account is mentioned in most articles on St. John Bosco. Ann Ball in her book Modern Saints, *Their Lives and Faces*, Book one, relates this tale.

Also, Rev. W. G. Austen S.D.B., mentions the wonderful and quite inexplicable appearances of Don Bosco's dog in an article he wrote that can be obtained from internet.

My own experience in Alaska was similar to Don Bosco's. It was in the dead of winter in the vicinity of Bethel, Alaska, on the Kuskaquim River. My companion and I traveled to Bethel regularly to teach the catechists.

It was about 9 o'clock one evening when we had just finished a very pleasant dinner with a local family. We commenced to walk back to our Quonset hut where we lived during these visits. It was extremely cold outside. The wind was blowing at about 10 or 15 m.p.h., which made the chill factor well below zero. The bits of icy snow particles stung our faces as we had to face the onslaught. With our trusty parkas a little closer to our faces we stepped out into the night.

Walking down the path I admired hearing the crunchy sound of the packed snow under our mukluk boots and seeing the beautiful light of the diamond-studded snow reflecting the half-moon.

As we proceeded I noticed that our little path was leading into the darkness of one of the wings of the local public school. The wing was built on stilts so the children could play outside even if there was rain. I was concerned because I was about to enter this very dark area and knew I wouldn't be able to see very well in the darkness. I said a short prayer for protection.

From the moon light and the one small light that lit up our

family's doorway, I could see several husky dogs that were tied up to their stakes. But what I witnessed next, I will never forget. There, standing next to the chained-up dogs, was the largest white dog I had ever seen. He was beautiful! He was as large or larger than a wolf. That was my first clue that there was something unusual about him because of his size and height.

Even though the white dog was standing next to the chained dogs, these dogs were totally unaware of his presence. In all the time of being a missionary in Alaska, working in various villages across the area, I noticed when a stray dog was loose and wandering near chained dogs, they would leap and lunge, barking furiously at any intruder on their property. In this case, the chained huskies did not even seem to know the white dog was there.

The beautiful white dog came towards me. He was very friendly and started to walk beside my friend and me on the snow-packed trail towards the deep shadows of the wing. I placed my left hand on the white dog's back. He was so large and tall, I didn't even have to bend over to let him lead me under the dark school wing. I remarked to my partner, "Isn't he beautiful!"

My third clue that this friend was "unearthly," was the length of his hair. The white dog had short fur. No short haired dog can survive the sub-zero cold winters of Alaska.

My fourth clue related again to his coat. In spite of having short fur, this dog was not trembling because of the cold. This beautiful white dog was warm to the touch. He led us out from under the dark school wing. As we were being led from the dark area below the stilted building, we could see a little because of the reflected light on the snow.

Suddenly we heard the voice of a man from behind a snowdrift to the right of the road. But in the blackened area my companion and I didn't know who the voice belonged to. What I deemed by now was that God in His mercy and goodness had sent me my guardian angel in disguise to protect and guide us home safely, so I mentally spoke to my angel that I heard a strange noise on my right. The massive white dog left my left hand and moved around to my right side to protect us from this strange noise. The beautiful white dog continued to walk at my right hand, placing himself between me and the snow banks along the path. As we walked closer to our Quonset hut, the little light at the door was becoming brighter. The comfort of our protector and this welcoming light in addition to the moon light made the continued walk easier.

I thanked my angel for his protection and for guiding us home. Suddenly the white dog backed up and disappeared totally and instantly. I looked around to see where he had gone. No animal can disappear so quickly and totally on the flat tundra. If this had been an earthly animal, we would have been able to see him for at least a hundred feet, but this beautiful white dog had just disappeared. To this date, I thank my beautiful and faithful angel friend and almighty God for taking such good care of us that evening, and for each day on our way to heaven.

ANGELIC WINGS OF CARE

Wings of care, Clouds of sky
Image you.
Round about—Gentle—Lightsome
Moved by the wind,
Moved by Ruah
Seen or not seen, They are!

Wings of care, curl round our souls
Our depths, now free
Delve into the heart of all.
World—Why are you?
Self—Who are you?
God—You are!

Angelic choice—Their fate settled
Unrepented, unrepeated.

Wings of care surround.
"Choose, choose life, not death.
Choose not self, broad way to death.
Choose Ruah, true way to life."

Wings of care,
Surround my sky.
May my inner eye see
Your wings powered
By Ruah's Love.
Around, above, beneath, beside
Carrying me Home.

(Ruah: Hebrew name for Spirit)
by Sister Mary Frances

WASHINGTON, D.C.

While I was studying clinical and counseling psychology at Catholic University, another incident took place that increased my gratitude to my God who sent His angels to protect me.

One early evening after dinner, all of the sisters were walking back from the university dining room. In the process, the other sisters left me to go to the library to pick up their books. I had taken my books to my room in the dorm which was another 4 blocks away from campus. Even though parts of Washington, D.C., are well known for crime, I thought I would be safe, because our dorm was very close to the campus.

I had only walked half a block alone when suddenly two men came out of an alley and started to follow me. I began to walk faster and faster praying for assistance. The men were still following me. I began to run. I raced across the street with the signal light that was green. When I got to the other side, suddenly I found myself surrounded by a dozen six-foot-tall men and another six men standing on the parking strip near the two men who had been following me. I don't know to this day what these men may have seen, maybe St. Michael the Archangel, but suddenly the dozen men parted and stepped back, made a path, to let me go through. I ran breathlessly into the dorm and upstairs to my room. A few minutes later I heard the screams coming from that same corner. I heard later that two other women were attacked on that corner by those men, but had been rescued by the campus police. It was a terrible experience for those two students. Again, I said a prayer of thanksgiving to the angels and my Lord for saving me.

INVISIBLE PRESENCE

Angels can protect even if one can't see them. I was working as a parish religious coordinator and attending meetings in Seattle. After a long evening meeting in Seattle, I prayed for protection and got into my little car to return home. As I stopped at a stoplight on a main street, a carload of young people came up behind me. As I looked into the vehicle through my rear view mirror, I recognized my nephew and his friends. The next day he called to ask, "Who was that big guy sitting next to you?"

I replied, "What fellow? I had no one else in the car with me."

My nephew insisted that he and his friends had seen a large man next to me in the front seat. There was no one with me driving back from Seattle. I am still convinced that he and his friends had seen my angel that evening.

THE ANGEL IN THE STORE

A different example of an angel taking on another form or disguise happened to me several years ago. A lovely young woman named Jo needed financial help and lived with us at the convent for a period of time. Jo, because of her gracious demeanor, got a job at a fancy restaurant in our town. She needed a black jacket, white blouse and a black matching skirt as a uniform. One of Jo's friend's, Pat, and I went shopping for clothes. Since we had a very limited budget, we were unable to find the appropriate clothes in regular department stores. After several unsuccessful hours of shopping, we stopped at the Salvation Army Store on our way home. This was our last hope. Jo might not be able to work unless she met the dress code. Before we went into the store, Pat and I said a prayer that the Lord would find us just what we wanted. Pat and I walked up and down the women's clothes racks and found a new white blouse in Jo's exact size. I found a nice black jacket, but no matching skirt. I looked up and saw a smiling face of a slender, not too rich looking man who said, "Extend your hand over to the left and you will find the skirt that will match that jacket."

I replied, amazed, "Thank you very much," and took his suggestion. I inserted my left hand into a crowded area of clothes that was half-hidden and pulled out the matching black skirt in Jo's size. I thanked the gentleman. Pat came over at that moment and I relayed the entire story to her. I wanted to point the man out to her, but he was gone! It all happened in only a few seconds, but he had disappeared!

We now had everything we had asked God to give us. Jo was elated to get the clothing so she could start her new job. Again we all gave thanks to God who takes care of little needs as well as big needs through his angels.

BREMERTON

As part of my healing ministry, I was asked to speak with Dr. Eugene Wiesner, Ph.D., at a workshop on the healing ministry. The workshop lasted all day and through the evening. Sister Gemma and I both stayed with a good friend at her apartment nearby.

After dinner, before the evening session was to begin, I went to the apartment and very carefully reviewed my notes, then placed all my evening hand written lecture notes into my pocket because I had such deep pockets in my jacket. I made sure the full packet of notes was right at the very bottom of that pocket. Having an outline available was very important to me so that I could be sure to cover all the pertinent material.

On my way back to the lecture hall with my friends, I stopped to check if my notes were still there, but they were gone! I had nothing in my pocket. Every single note had vanished. I said a fervent prayer, "Jesus, help. Find my notes, please!" No sooner was that prayer mentally said when a tall young gentleman came running over the hill, ran past my friends, and handed me my treasured notes. This unknown man said, "Here are the notes you wanted, Sister." He walked quickly away, back over that same hill. I was then able to give the talk that evening with great assurance. Once again, I thanked my beloved angel for being right there, taking good care of my every need.

THE EVENTFUL NIGHT

That same evening after the lecture, Sister Gemma and I returned to our friend's apartment, shared our experiences, relaxed and retired to bed for a much needed rest. An hour later I woke with a start. There was a loud banging and thumping noise from inside the wall. I said a short prayer for protection, "Dear heavenly Father, in Jesus' name, I humbly ask you for continued protection from all evil forces." Then I mentally said, "Evil spirits of useless noise, I command you in the name of Jesus to be bound and go to Jesus Christ and He will know what to do with you, and don't come back."

All the loud knocking ceased immediately and I went back to sleep. A few hours later, I was awakened by more knocking and thumping coming from inside the walls. I knew it wasn't the same evil spirit "creep" that I had already sent off to Jesus to be disposed of. So I said the same silent prayer for protection and gave the same command for the evil angel or demon to go to Jesus. All the noise and banging ceased again. This same experience continued through the night until all the evil spirits were bound and sent to Jesus.

The next morning, I asked Sister Gemma if she had heard anything during the night. She replied, "Did I!" The noise and banging kept me from sleeping a good part of the night. I didn't elaborate on the subject for fear of frightening her unduly.

After we returned home, we got a phone call from our Bremerton friend where we had stayed. She joyfully shared that a Satanic coven which had met every week in the apartment above her suddenly moved out permanently. Praise the Lord! She didn't tell or warn us beforehand because she didn't want to scare us. Maybe it was just as well. We again thanked God who had taken such good care of us.

THE NIGHT ADVENTURE

A similar incident occurred at a new house that our order had purchased next to the novitiate. The expansion was necessary because the numbers of novices and postulants were increasing.

The sisters asked me to teach the novices courses in Theology and Scripture. The superior assigned me the master bedroom of the new house to stay in as my living quarters. Every time I entered my room, I got a very uneasy feeling. I felt an ominous presence of a person in the middle of the room who resented my being there. Night after night I heard knocking right beside me. Each time I would ask God, my angel and especially St. joseph to guard me. I then proceeded to command the evil spirit or departed soul to stop the useless racket and leave.

But what really convinced me that something preternatural (dealing with spirits) was really going on was when the sisters who had taken vows had a late party of ice-cream and cake at the main novitiate building. We dispersed at 10 P.M. and I started to walk along a spot-lighted path through a small section of woods separating the two buildings. I felt uneasy going by myself, so I called our two strapping police dogs to accompany me. These dogs were truly protective of the sisters. In fact, only the day before they had bitten a man who trespassed on the property. The bite was severe enough to send him to the hospital. So with one police dog on either side of me, I felt brave. But as the dogs and I came onto the newly acquired property, i saw a "cloudy" being walking towards me on the path. This "being" scattered the fallen leaves with each step. As the "being" walked, the sound of the scrunched leaves was audible as well.

I looked at the two "ferocious" police dogs for their protection and to my utter amazement, both dogs put their tails between their legs and bounded in the opposite direction, back toward their dog houses at the main novitiate building, leaving me unprotected. Fine guard dogs they were! I was disgusted.

As the shuffled steps continued to come closer to me, I put my trusty door key in my hand and I ran the fastest tenth of a mile of my life. I bounded up the steps, taking them two or three at a time and put my key into the lock. It didn't work! I took it out and turned the key over to try it again. At the same time, I looked over my shoulder as the leaves continued to rustle and the "being" continued toward me. I said a desperate short prayer, "Jesus, Mary, Joseph, save me!" All of a sudden, the door swung open by itself and I ran in and slammed the door closed. I ran up the stairs. Some of the novices came out into the hallway to see what was wrong. "Are you okay?" they asked.

I replied that all was well and excused myself for disturbing the peace. I didn't tell them what had happened.

The next day, I related my experience to the superior, especially about the ominous presence in the master bedroom. She told me, "The sister who was in your room before you said the same thing."

I thought to myself as I left her office, "Good, I wasn't the only one to have that eerie experience." This made me question what unusual things had occurred here in this house.

Shortly after the incident I was transferred to a parish. In the meantime, the whole novitiate was moved. I lost track of whether or not that master bedroom and the house were ever exorcised.

SKIING "LIFT"

Sometimes angels come to our rescue by physically picking us up and putting us somewhere else. A sister and I were offered a free skiing trip if we chaperoned a bus load of teens. This particular evening was very cold, but very clear and beautiful. You could easily see the twinkling lights of Vancouver below us and all the lights along the ocean shore.

Sister and I skied slowly and carefully down the hill a dozen times, and this particular time we grabbed the T-Bar, which acts as a substitute chair lift. Sister landed incorrectly on the bar and accidentally got her ski caught over a narrow icy mound grooved out by many preceding skiers. Her ski suddenly landed on top of my ski and foot. We were starting to lose our balance and fall off the T-Bar. I called out to ask if she could move her ski off mine, but before she could answer, we both fell forward into the icy snow. My face was in the crusty, icy snow and I caught my ski at a 45 degree angle in the moving T-Bar. As the T-Bar moved up the hill, it was doubling my back in two. I was afraid that my back would be broken. I panicked and called out in great distress, "O Sacred Heart, save me!"

The Lord heard my anguished prayer and my angel lifted both of us!

The angel instantly placed us gently about fifteen feet from the T-bar groove onto the softest bed of fluffy new snow. There we sat, safe and sound away from all the danger. The sudden release of the T-Bar caused the taut cable to swing back and forth. All the skiers on the T-Bar who had watched in horror the accidental fall, suddenly saw us on the snowy ground ten to fifteen feet away. They all had their mouths open and stared at us as they passed us by. As sister and I were sitting in the snow, we realized that in the excitement we had both lost our ski poles, but we found them a few feet away stuck together in the snow. We thanked our faithful angel friends and most of all, our Lord, for our rescue.

BABY IN THE SEATTLE ARENA

Sisters Noreen, Frances and I attended the Northwest Charismatic Conference at the Seattle Sports Arena some years ago. The entire event was memorable because of the wonderful speakers and music. It was even more memorable, because of the miracle of a small baby and an angel.

There were many chairs on the floor of the sports arena and three floors of bleachers up to the very top level of the arena. Everything was built over a floor of hard cement. One of my teacher friends was seated in the top bleacher section with her five young children. Despite her watchfulness, the two year old climbed to the very top of the section, to the very top bench, where there was no guard rail. We were on the opposite side of the arena and gasped, in unison, as we watched the little boy crawl closer and closer to the edge. We all prayed, "Oh Lord, send your angels to catch him in Jesus' name!" Our prayer was answered, for as he slipped off the edge, falling three stories (60 feet) toward the cement floor, he was stopped in mid air. About two feet above the cement floor the angel(s) gently placed him on his feet upright on the hard floor. His mother rushed down to his side, and hugged her child. Both were crying after the harrowing experience. There wasn't a single scratch on him. God is so good!

AGLOW MEETING

Sister Mary Frances and I were invited to a Women Aglow meeting. After the meeting's guest speaker had finished her testimony, she came over to our section during prayer time. She asked us to pray with her for several things. I reminded her that we couldn't do the healing, but that God could heal anything. Sometimes He answers our sincere prayers with a yes, quickly, sometimes slowly, and once in awhile He has to say no. But if He has to say no, He will always do something better in its place. The speaker nodded in agreement and we prayed with fervor to the Lord.

Just as I thought we were finished, in my spirit, I saw darkness come towards her. I thought to myself, "Oh, oh!" We had better pray this one out."

Without frightening her, I gently said, "Maybe we could pray for special protection for you and your family." So we prayed for that protection.

A few hours later, the Aglow President called us with such enthusiasm and joy. She related that when the speaker got home, her son called and told her how he had just ridden his motorcycle in Seattle, when a vehicle came out unexpectedly from a side street and hit him and his motorcycle so hard that it set him catapulting up into the air. As he was falling, he was caught by what he called an invisible "arm" and was put down gently to the ground without injury. His motorcycle was totally destroyed. The police could hardly believe it. The young man didn't have even a scratch.

We all gave praise to the Lord and His protective angels.

A VICTORY INCIDENT

The power of prayer in the name of Jesus was never so evident as the time when Sister Mary Frances and I were asked to give an all day retreat for all the young people before they left for Denver, Colorado, to visit the Pope.

We brought our two Shi Tsu dogs with us. While the retreat was going on, the dogs were sound asleep at our feet with their leashes on to prevent them from running round and being a nuisance.

One session of the retreat was entitled, "Choose Life, not Death," as mentioned in Exodus, and in that talk there was a section based upon St. Ignatius Loyola's description of heaven and hell, and of the two camps or standards.

Sister Frances described heaven and how beautiful it is: There is total love, happiness, color, joy, light, fragrances, beautiful music, beauty, sheer selflessness, and best of all, our God of love. Then I gave St. Ignatius' rendition of hell, a state of total hopelessness, despair, total hatred, ugliness, and darkness. Just as I began describing hell, suddenly a dark form appeared in the back of the room. I could feel the ominous hatred coming from it, threatening to come forward, as if to harm us.

Our two little dogs woke up out of their sound sleep and leapt up into the air, tugging at the ends of their leashes, snarling and growling at this dark form. Having experienced a similar thing in Medford, Oregon at a parish mission, Sister Frances and I both prayed for the full armor of protection of the Blessed Trinity, God's angels and God's saints for everyone present and for those at home. Then I gave a quiet, but firm, order, "I command you in Jesus' holy name to be bound and quietly go to Jesus to be disposed of according to His will."

At that order, the evil one disappeared. Our little dogs came back, curled up at our feet again and went back to sleep. Most of the young people present and their chaperons, (except for a couple of people) saw this dark form. It was a very important lesson for everyone. It taught the importance of the full armor of prayer for protection. The effective command, "In God's holy name," is infinitely more powerful than any creature. When we went back for a visit, we were told that they were still talking about this amazing incident.

In a time when everything is rationalized, some people have difficulty believing that there are bad angels, let alone any angels at all. Pope Leo XIII in 1884 had a frightening experience. After saying Mass in his private Vatican chapel, it was said that he lapsed into, what appeared to be, a coma. After he regained his composure, he startled everyone by stating solemnly, "What a terrible scene I saw!"

Later Pope Leo XIII described what he had heard, the sound of the demons' guttural voices and especially that of Satan boasting to God that he could destroy the Catholic Church and bring the whole world to hell if he were given sufficient time and power, approximately 75 to 100 years. Even Satan had to ask God for permission. If the devil couldn't accomplish this in that allotted time he would go down in defeat.

The vision gave the pope the inspiration to compose the very powerful prayer to the archangel Michael to be said each day.

"St. Michael the Archangel, defend us against the enemy, safeguard us against the wickedness and snares of the devil. May God rebuke him, we humbly pray, and do thou, O Prince of the Heavenly Host, by the power of God, cast into hell Satan and all the other evil spirits who prowl about the world seeking the ruin of souls. Amen."

This story is recorded in the records of Pope Leo XIII and also under any explanation of how the prayer to Saint Michael came to be written. Our Lady of Sorrows Church has this explanation on internet.

Even though we don't say this powerful prayer for protection after every Mass as a formal prayer, as directed in the past by Pope Leo XIII, we can do very well to say it for protection especially in the morning along with the Morning Offering.

I have added a very important and powerful prayer for protection. Many people have asked for such a prayer, and Biblical sources.

MORNING PRAYER
FOR PROTECTION

EPH. 6 . . . "Be strong in the Lord and in the strength of His might. Put on the whole armor of God, that you may be able to stand against the attacks of the devil. Therefore take on the whole armor of God."

PETER 5:8 . . . "Satan is like a roaring lion roaming around the world seeking those whom he could devour. Resist him and he will run away from you."

JESUS Mark 5:36/Luke 21:36; 22:40 . . . "Not to be afraid but pray, be spiritually prepared." . . . "Fear is useless. What is needed is trust."

LET US PRAY

Dear Heavenly Father, through the Hearts of Jesus and Mary, in and with the Holy Spirit, I humbly ask of you for that full armor of protection against all evil powers, visible or invisible. I ask this protection not only for myself but for all my loved ones, pets, vehicles, property, home and everything in it.

And if there be any hexes, spells, or curses thrown at me or my loved ones, etc. I ask that these curses be cast back at the perpetrators a hundredfold, not to destroy but to convert and save.

Thank you, Lord God, for hearing my fervent prayer in Jesus Christ's holy name. Amen.

P.S. (Full armor means the full protection of the Blessed Trinity, all the angels and saints, and Our Blessed Mother, given to us at the foot of the cross to be our Spiritual Mother.)

QUESTION—DID I EVER SEE MY GUARDIAN ANGEL?

While in a certain beautiful town in Washington as Religious Education Coordinator, I kept out of mischief with so many meetings, teacher trainings, home visitations, bible classes, etc. that the only quiet time available for holy hour each day was between 11 P.M. and 1 A.M. There was great joy in being in a dark chapel with only the sanctuary lamp to light up the tabernacle.

One night when I was praying and looking at the tabernacle, I became aware of something unusual. I saw my silhouette on the right side of the chapel wall. That's strange, I thought. That's impossible because the source of light was only from the sanctuary lamp next to the tabernacle in the front of the chapel, but the source of the silhouette came from behind me and to my left. I turned and there was a beautiful soft glow of light from what I believe was my guardian angel. My thanks were profuse for his being there with me, helping me to pray. This happened several dozen times and on a few occasions the whole chapel was lit up. At the time I longed for my beloved Trinity, and I desired heaven so very much, that they took pity on my weaknesses. Praise God.

THE SHIP EXPERIENCE

Sister Frances and I and a friend, on our way to an art show, stopped to eat lunch at a little restaurant. While we were eating our clam chowder, I finally noticed two people looking at us. They came over and introduced themselves and asked if I was a Catholic nun. I nodded, yes. They said they had noticed my veil and made the decision to come over for a bit. "We have a few questions to ask," they said. That bit of time lasted an hour and a half. The people were fallen-away Catholics. They had just recently begun to think seriously about life, goals, and destiny. They insisted we come over to their house for dinner. Several weeks later we went to see them again. The couple found out I enjoyed fishing and they promptly invited me to go fishing with them at a future time.

Several weeks later, while I was in chapel, I received a very late telephone call from this couple. They asked if I wanted to go fishing the following day. To my amazement my calendar showed that this was the only clear day in the month. I told them I would love to go along with them, and we arranged a time to meet at the Dungeness Spit. After returning to the chapel I returned to prayer. I suddenly saw myself in their little boat with a huge ocean faring ship bearing down upon us. The ship hit us and we landed in the water. I was hurt. That was a strange distraction and I shook it off, attributing it to my wandering imagination and went on trying to finish my prayers. Again, the same scene came to me; the ocean faring ship hitting us and all of us falling into the water. Since this happened three different times that evening, I thought that it might be a sign that maybe I shouldn't go, but on the other hand, the family would need a warning to protect them.

The next morning was a spectacularly beautiful and clear day with the sun forming little diamonds on the ocean waters. It was a perfect fishing day.

The couple and I launched the eighteen-foot boat at the east side of Dungeness Spit. The woman told me as I arrived, "Sister, we are so glad to have you come with us." I replied that for more than one reason, I too, was very glad to be included on this excursion.

They were taking their two grandchildren with them on this trip. It took us some time to get around the end of the seven-mile spit. They turned off the big engine and started up the small troller engine. We were at all parts of the boat, putting bait on, hooks, lures and lead sinkers. We cast our fishing lines and enjoyed the panoramic view of the Olympic mountains. Even then I was praying about the anticipated accident.

What happened next is something that I will never forget. Suddenly a foreboding wall of thick fog came upon us from the northwest and engulfed our little boat so completely that it obliterated any sign of land, water or sun. It is a fog that fishermen dread.

The man decided it would be a passing thing and continued to troll what he thought was a straight safe course. For about a half hour this tense situation continued. That is, the situation was tense for me.

Suddenly my angel said to me, "Watch the horizon!" and so I did. I felt like one of those radar devices on boats that whirl around and around. The children and the couple were busy checking their fishing lines, when to my horror coming at us was a huge ocean freighter— three stories high. The gigantic black hull was blotting out the faint disk of the sun. I yelled, "A ship! Can you steer out of the way?"

The man jumped up and opened the canopy to start the big engine, then thought better of it. There could be real danger of an explosion. In the meantime I could see the gigantic bow of the freighter bearing down upon our little eighteen-foot boat. If it ever hit us, the freighter crew would never even know they ran into anything. Because we were so small, it would be like a mosquito bite-or a small thud of a half sunken log under the ship.

I could see that ominous high wall of water that was created as the freighter came closer and closer to us. The children were now yelling and crying. The man rushed back to the idling troller motor and tried to turn the steering throttle to the left. Our little boat began to respond just as we were several feet from the bow of the freighter. In desperation I turned my head away in self defense, to avoid seeing the horrible impact of the freighter. I prayed, "Lord, dear angels, help!"

A miracle occurred. The man finally managed with great effort to turn our little boat to the left even more as we barely missed the huge hull of the freighter literally by inches. We looked up and saw a look-out sailor with his tam and turtleneck sweater, with folded arms, looking at us, but not moving. Next we saw the gigantic anchor dangling from its hole with a lot of rusty nails cascading down the side. It seemed an eternity as the first huge set of cranes went by, then the second set, the third, and the fourth and finally the housing. To my horror, I was staring at an impressive and frightening set of propellers. If our little boat ever got too close to those blades, we would be ground up into mincemeat. But an invisible hand kept us from being sucked in. Praise God.

For a long time after the ship had finally gone past, we bounced on the wake of waves left by the mammoth ship. We heaved a sigh of relief and we thanked God for saving us. I said, "That was why I came, besides the fishing and enjoying your good company."

The children said, "Maybe we should go back to catechism."

The wife told her husband, "Honey, maybe we, too, should go back to church and the practice of our faith. The Lord must have spared us for something."

When the fog lifted enough for us to see the shoreline, we realized then, that we had wandered into the ocean shipping lanes without knowing it.

After getting back into my car my legs felt rather wobbly. How could I ever thank the Lord and His angels enough for saving us!

THE LOG

On many occasions, as a catechetical teacher trainer, I made monthly trips to the west end of the Olympic Peninsula. On this particular trip, the evening meeting and instructions ended quite late. It is rewarding to do God's work. It is rewarding to see teachers gain assurance and competence in their classroom work.

Sister Margaret had come to keep me company. After the meeting, we dashed to our car because the rain was pouring down. "So hard and heavy it was raining everything but cats and dogs." We recited our car prayer for protection and we started on our way home.

In my eagerness to get home, I was over driving my head-lights, especially on a long straight stretch of road. Suddenly my headlights reflected a large log in the road, blocking the entire width on both sides. Sister and I both gasped and once again we said a short prayer—very short—"Lord!"

And the Lord in His love and mercy again sent His angels. Suddenly the log was gone! The angels had lifted the log and placed it to the side of the road. Sister and I continued to drive along, saying prayers of thanksgiving.

The next time I went out to that area I deliberately looked for that log and found it. The log was still parallel to the highway. Thank you, dear Lord and dear angels.

"CARVE IT, I'LL HELP YOU"

In a small town in western Montana, Sister Mary Frances, Paddy, and I were conducting a prayer workshop for the parishioners. While Paddy and I were alternating giving the presentations, Sister Frances was whittling on an attractive piece of wood. Father Michael, the pastor who was standing in the back of the room, was observing the wood carving activity with great interest. He then disappeared into his office and brought out a beautiful twelve inch pewter statue of the holy family.

Father Michael stunned all three of us by asking Sister Mary Frances to reproduce the pewter statue into a six-foot high wood statue of Joseph, Mary and Jesus that he was planning for the front of the church.

Sister very politely responded that we were only amateurs and could only carve flats and not rounds. Again after one of the talks, Father Michael broached the subject of the monumental carving.

Paddy and I were utterly astounded by what came from Sister Mary Frances' lips. "Father, we'll do it."

After sister's unexpected consent, we cornered her during lunch time. "An explanation, please, especially when our efforts and valuable time were volunteered without any of our input."

She replied, "While you two were giving the last talk, I went to the Lord for direction. 'What do You want, oh, Lord.' I heard distinctly His words, 'Tell Father that you will carve it. I will help you.' So what was I to do?"

Paddy and I acquiesced at that point, but I had to tease her concerning one of our unwritten guidelines of discernment, especially when the decision included more than one person. She looked a little sheepish, but reminded us that she had received very encouraging words from Jesus as she had prayed for guidance.

Several days later after arriving back home, a good sized truck backed up to our convent basement door with what looked like a six-foot by three-foot by one-foot piece of white fir. It felt damp to the touch. It was mammoth!

Undaunted we commenced our "We Project," as it came to be called. Where did we start first? We prayed! So, using the little pewter statue that Father Michael loaned us, I mathematically produced a six-foot sketch which we proceeded to carbon-trace the three figures on the fir wood; and then had our very good friend, Chet, chain-saw the main outline; all of which saved a lot of time and wear and tear on our small tools.

After several months of interruptions, meetings and delays it was decided that Sister Frances would carve the child Jesus, Paddy would carve Our Blessed Lady, and, because I was the tallest, I would carve St. Joseph.

Sister Mary Frances lamented, "I am really having trouble with baby Jesus. St. Joseph looked tall and handsome. Our Lady looked peaceful and beautiful. But baby Jesus' face, which should have been oval and shaped like an egg, was getting rounder and rounder. Heavens! Jesus now looked as though he had mumps! "Lord, you said You'd help—well, help!" Sister Frances prayed. Two days later on the feast of Saint Joseph, two Dominican sisters, Bertand and Mary, came to our house for supper and a visit. The three of us described vividly the whole story of our "We Project" to our visiting sisters. They looked it over and at each other and Sister Mary said, "It so happens that we are woodcarvers. We'd love to help."

They were real woodcarvers! As they skillfully carved the features of the holy family, it began to resemble the original pewter model. All of us, especially Sister Frances, prayed a thanksgiving prayer. "Thank you, Lord. You said you'd help. You didn't say how."

The five of us, now in real earnest, were busy causing the wood curls to fly. Father Michael called on the phone for the first time, inquiring how the statue was progressing. I answered with relief that it was coming along just fine.

After being assured that the carving would actually be

completed, Father related to me that a lady in the parish was donating $10,000 for a statue in memory of her recently deceased brother. This was to be divided and shared by the five carvers with the principal amount going for the many needs of the parish. This was a welcome surprise.

We really worked steadily from then on and were so pleased to see the "We Project" coming ever closer to a truly artistic conclusion in the midst of all those shavings and sawdust.

In June a stately statue depicting the standing, smiling Saint Joseph, and Our Blessed Lady holding the child Jesus was strapped securely to the top of the station wagon and all ready to travel to Montana.

It was dedicated with all the parishioners and townspeople participating, including us Washingtonians. Judging by the smiles of satisfaction of everyone and the many compliments, it was a true blessing for all. We all gave thanksgiving to God, still remembering His words, "Carve it. I'll help you." This experience was a real walk of trust with listening ears and willing hearts.

THE MIRACLE OF THE
RUPTURED AORTA

It is well known that in answer to sincere, trusting and persevering prayer, God, in His love and mercy, can move hearts as well as mountains. That was exactly what happened in a small western town.

All the priests at our parish were going to a Deanery meeting and they weren't available when our local Catholic surgeon called for help and prayer for a patient undergoing a most serious surgery at the hospital. Deeply concerned, the surgeon had his nurse call me at the convent and explained the urgency of the situation. I said I would be right there. The drive was a short one. I parked the old car near the hospital emergency room door and ran directly into the operating room. A nurse helped me scrub my hands, put on a surgical gown and a facial mask. I had never been in an operating room to pray for anyone, and I couldn't help wonder about the final outcome. The nurse ushered me into the operating suite. There were tubes everywhere, some with blood running through and some with a clear liquid. I took care to cautiously step over and around all the sophisticated equipment. The surgeon and the surgical assistant greeted me with a nod. The staff stepped back as I walked up to a large man lying on the operating table. I was startled. His chest was wide open and I could see his heart!

The heart monitor showed a straight line. I thought to myself. "Oh, Lord, Oh! What do I do now because the doctors and nurses will want me to do something immediately. I had better make this prayer a short, short one. But what should I pray, oh Lord?" On inspiration, I traced the sign of the cross on the ill man's forehead, praying at the same time, "Oh God, Our Father, in Jesus' name, according to your holy will, please make him well. Please guide the hands of the doctors and give the patient peace. Amen. Thank you Lord."

Immediately after the prayer, I noticed the heart monitor beep and show a heart beat line once again. A prayer of thanksgiving filled my heart. The doctors and the nurses nodded again with smiles this time.

After returning the gown and mask to a nurse, I left the surgical area and went to console and pray with the patient's family.

The family was visiting the Pacific Northwest from California when the father had his attack. After conversing and praying with the family, I left the hospital a bit shaken.

The next day I went to the hospital to visit my patient. I found him doing well. Several days later, I again returned to the hospital, but my patient was not in his room. My immediate fear was that he had died, but the nurse at the station told me joyfully that he and his family had returned to California that day. Before he left, the man had left me a word of grateful thanks for the miracle. This time it was my turn to joyfully give thanks to almighty God who does all things well. To this day I wonder whether the man had been clinically dead. He may very well have been.

Years later, when seeking confirmation for this story, I was informed by the surgeon, that this man hadn't suffered a heart attack, but rather it was a burst aorta. I was amazed that he remembered the case and the date as well.

While telling this story to some friends who were nurses, they exclaimed that there were only two or three cases in the world in which someone survived a burst aorta! We all marveled at the wonderful works of God.

TWO MIRACLES (BACK TO BACK)

At the Northwest Charismatic Conference Sister Frances and I were part of a healing prayer team. A man came up to us in the hall after one general session and asked us to pray for his twenty-year-old son who had a very serious illness which left him paralyzed. The young man was leaning far to one side in his wheelchair. Sister and I brought the young man and his parents into a quiet room. We asked this very ill person if he believed that Jesus could heal him. He said, "Yes."

I then asked the young man's permission to place our hands on his head. Sister Frances and I very gently positioned our hands on his head, just as Jesus did in blessing the children, and the blind man. We prayed to God the Father in Jesus' holy name for peace of mind and body. We then asked for a healing of the young man's serious illness.

Just as we completed our short prayer, several women

came into the room looking for us. They were pulling their friend, who was yelling and screaming and greatly agitated. The two women looked at us and pleaded for help for their friend.

What should we do? Remembering Ephesians, Chapter 6, I prayed fervently, "Dear heavenly Father, in Jesus' holy name, we humbly ask you for the full armor of protection against all evil forces visible or invisible, not only for ourselves but also for all our loved ones, our brothers and sisters, our property, homes, all that is in our homes, pets and vehicles, everything." We then silently asked Jesus to reveal what was really bothering this poor woman. Both Sister and I discerned in our spirits that she was angry, fearful and had great difficulty forgiving those who had hurt her. We quietly commanded, "In the name of Jesus Christ the son of the living God, we command you evil spirits of excess anger, of fear and of lack of forgiveness to be silent, now!"

Immediately there was a dead silence in the room. What a relief! I glanced around to look at the boy in the wheelchair. He and his parents had disappeared from the room. Sister and I continued to give our full attention to this woman before us. She was now quiet, but still agitated.

After asking the Lord for guidance and protection, we again commanded the evil spirits of useless anger, fears and lack of forgiveness. "Leave this lady and go to Jesus Christ. Jesus will know what to do with you. You must leave now and don't come back."

The woman immediately calmed down and a real change

took place. She sank down into a chair that was near her. She sat there and looked like she had just come out of a bad dream. There was a peaceful expression on her face. For the first time since she had come into that room, her friends could let go of her. Everyone was relieved by the new peacefulness. Every one of us said a prayer of praise and gratitude to God, and then departed for the next general session.

Later that weekend, after leaving a meeting, a young woman came running over and grabbed us. "Do you remember me, Sisters? I'm the one that you prayed for. I feel wonderful and so happy and free!"

We listened in awe to her story. We tactfully reminded her of what Jesus said about the importance of "decorating the house" of her soul; of daily prayer, good works, abundant use of the mass and sacraments, avoiding the near occasions of sin, and joining, if possible a spiritual support group. Her two friends came over, beaming and looking admiringly at their transformed friend. We all gave the glory to the Lord for his love and mercy. We asked St. Michael and his angels to continue to guard them from now on.

As a sequel one might ask, "What happened to the crippled young man in the wheelchair?" Many times we don't hear about the miracles of healing until months or years later. But in this particular case, we did have the joy of learning what happened.

Two years later at another conference a young man came running over to Sister Frances and myself all excited. "Do you remember me, Sisters?" I, for one, confessed that I did not. He, with a big smile, said, "I was the crippled fellow in the wheelchair in Spokane. Right after the prayer, I began to feel so much better and to the doctor's amazement he found nothing wrong with me. I'm attending the university getting my M.A. degree. I thank God and you for your loving prayers."

God is so good.

DO ANGELS HAVE NAMES?

Do angels have names? They do have names given them by God; for example, Michael, meaning "who is like God," the leader of the angels, who with God's power, vanquished Lucifer and his disobedient, prideful angels to Hell. Michael is the protector of the Church.

Then we have another powerful angel mentioned in the Old Testament, Raphael, which means, "God heals." We can see this beautiful angel extolled in the Book of Tobit. He is the guardian on the journey. He is the healer. He expelled demons. He is one of the seven angels who offered the prayers of Tobit to Almighty God. Finally, the angel went on an errand collecting money for Tobit's son.

Lastly, Gabriel, meaning, "God is strong." Gabriel is one of the seven Archangels who stand before God. In the book of Daniel, (Dan. 8:16-26), he explained visions and he also made announcements to Zechariah, Mary and Joseph.

The angel Gabriel has the unique honor of being connected with the messianic fulfillment. He was one of the many angels who were truly faithful to almighty God.

It took about five years of humble and persistent asking in prayer for my guardian angel in his friendship to reveal his name. The waiting helped me learn to be more patient. It was a fourfold gift.

Early one Sunday morning, just before dawn, I heard God the Father's voice speaking to my heart and soul, accepting once again my love and consecration; then God the Son repeating the same thing but adding He had me in His Sacred Heart; then in an ethereal voice, the Holy Spirit, the gentle gift of God the Father and God the Son, came upon my heart and possessed me even more deeply and filled me with a deep joy and comfort. Finally, my angel said clearly, "My name is Marlin, which means 'Sea full of love.'" Then total silence. So much to think about! So much to thank the blessed Trinity for. It came at just the right time! I needed this extra boost for my spirit.

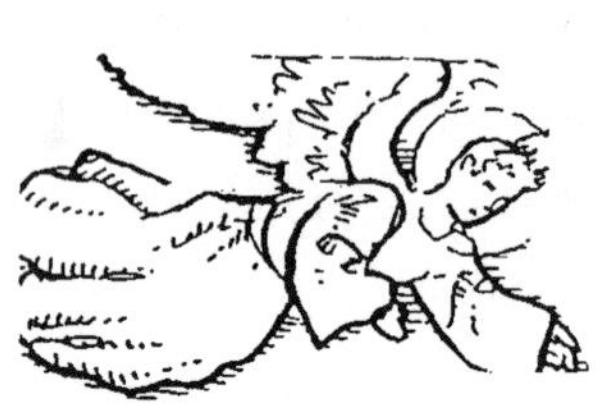 

OUR ANGEL TRAVELERS

Sister Mary Frances and I saved our pennies and had received special gifts from our friends over the years anticipating a trip to Leichester, England for a General Assembly. We decided to take this occasion to travel to Ireland, Scotland and Wales before the assembly began. After the assembly we planned to travel to France, Portugal, and Belgium.

While visiting the famous castle in Edinburgh, and especially the little chapel, we were told that this was the special place where the queen used to pray. I walked toward the small table located at the front. I prayed interiorly to the Queen of Scots, St. Margaret. Quite unexpectedly I experienced her strong presence. I was filled with such joy! What a privilege to make that little visit. The little stone chapel was practically the only edifice that the attacking enemy armies left intact. They destroyed everything else.

After that special pilgrimage we went to Grimsby to another sisters' house and found out that the British rail company changed its schedules and so missed the train ride through Wales. To top off everything we were told the ferry boat company was still on strike.

So after Mass, we mentioned our predicament at the breakfast table. The sisters smiled and said, "You won't guess, but our pastor is planning to drive over to Wales to catch the ferry over to Lochadaire, Ireland."

We were blessed to see the countryside by car. In fact we were so close to the wall of one castle that we could roll down the car windows and touch the cold stones.

We reached the ferry boat landing and found out that the ferry strike was over, to our delight and relief. Thus, we would be arriving at our prearranged bed & breakfast as originally planned.

When we disembarked in Ireland, we looked around for the gentleman who was to meet us with the appropriate B&B sign. Interiorly again, I asked St. Raphael to help us find him, and no sooner was that silent prayer said, when we turned and there he was with a sign and a smile.

At the breakfast table the next morning we asked about how to reach Dublin, so we could charter a four-seater single engine Cessna airplane. We were amazed to learn that our friends' cousins were visiting Ireland at the same time, and invited Sister Mary Frances and me to join them. So instead of riding in a bus, we rode with them in their rented car to Dublin. It was an impressive city with many people drawing chalk pictures on the plaza stones, musicians singing and dancing to entertain the public, and many beautiful churches.

It was fascinating to visit the genealogy center across from the Trinity University grounds. Its well kept records helped us to realize that my father's side of the family had its varied personages and an interesting coat of arms.

At the Dublin Airport, to our delight, there was a small plane charter service open. After negotiations, I shared with the pilot that I had my pilot's license. He said with a big smile, "I'll make you an official member of the Irish Flying Club and let you do the flying and at half-price." That sounded like a splendid idea to me, since my brother was donating the pennies to make this flight possible.

After we had our pilot pre-check completed, we taxied slowly toward the takeoff point and then waited our turn. When the light turned green, I gunned the engine, got momentum, and we were officially off the runway. After the 45 degree turn we aimed toward the west and the coast of Ireland. It was breathtaking. We could see all the varied shades and tints of green. No wonder they called Ireland the "emerald isle."

At 500 feet, I ventured to look around. It was truly beautiful—a canal, people working in their fields, and others cutting out squares of peat for winter fuel. Sister excitedly said, "Look, a castle! Could we get a better look at it?" Without losing altitude, we tipped a wing for a better look.

There were also several watchtowers, reminiscent of years of people being watchful over property and lives.

I noticed at the beginning of the trip that there was an unusually high ominous black cloud stacking up in the north west quadrant. As a precaution we flew over the Killarney Lakes and landed at Shannon Airport. We ate a quick lunch and then took off again after checking in our adjusted flight plan with the flight officials. This time we flew in a southeast direction, taking the flight south of the mountain of multi-colors, flying low over the cream-tinted sandy beaches and estuaries. While we were flying toward our destination near Rosalaire, I glanced over my shoulder and saw that the 50,000-foot dark purple-black wall of storm was menacingly approaching ever closer. After we landed safely on a short grassy airfield at Wexford, we said a thankful good-bye to our most cordial pilot. As we watched him and his little plane take off, we said a fervent prayer, asking God and his angels to protect him all the way back to Dublin.

When safe and sound at the local Rosalaire bed & breakfast, the anticipated storm hit. Everything broke loose! It looked as though we were in a bathysphere under the ocean waves. There was thunder and lightning and even some hail at first.

The next day we got on the ferry that was destined for Fishguard, Wales. We thought this ride was going to be quiet and peaceful, but no sooner were we into our reading matter when a husband and his wife sat down across from us and struck up a conversation. They found out that we were on our way to London via British rail. They insisted that we travel with them via Southampton, England. After a delightful lunch and a longer than expected trip to Southampton, we said good-bye to our new-found friends and took a late train to London. While on route, we took one look at the wall map of the multiple underground tubes of London. We gasped, and then said a wee prayer, "Lord, we will get lost for sure. Please send help. Thanks, for hearing our prayer."

A lovely looking lady got on our almost empty train and sat next to sister and myself. I ventured to ask her for help. We told her that the sisters at the convent across from St. James Catholic church had invited us to stay with them overnight and we didn't have the faintest idea what tube to take or how far to travel on it. She smiled and replied that she was going to London to pick up her car and that she was going on the exact subway train in the exact subway tube and would be going just one stop beyond our stop. A coincidence? I don't think so; not after seeing the maze of possible ways to get lost.

As we were getting closer to our destination she led us off the train and pointed, "Go up those steps, hail the taxi that is there at the top and go to the sisters' convent only a few blocks away." We thanked her profusely and hurriedly went up the steps, and sure enough there was only one taxi and it seemed to be waiting just for us. It was a very wise and good thing that we had called ahead to notify the sisters of our late arrival.

After ringing the night bell, we heard the steps of the sister who was waiting up for us. It was with a look of relief she let us in. We shared our adventures over a cup of tea, before going to the chapel for a short visit of thanksgiving for the safe trip.

After the general assembly meeting, Sister Mary Frances and I had the wonderful opportunity to visit Lisieux, where St. Therese hallowed the town by her humble way of living and her dedication to her beloved Jesus. Later on in the day after we attended the mass in the basement of the basilica, we proceeded to Rennes, France, where a French family was in anticipation of our arrival by train. It was interesting how we managed to communicate with our French family considering our questionable French vocabulary.

The next morning, after a most welcome rest under a gigantic goose-down blanket, we sat down at the dining room table wondering what to do next, for placed before each of us was a medium-sized bowl with hot coffee mixed with a lot of milk. Sister Mary Frances signaled to me, "What do we do with it? Spoon it, drink it, or what?"

"Watch Monsieur Babin," I quietly whispered.

Sure enough, he sensed our predicament, picked up his trusty French bun, and dunked it into the coffee milk. With relief and mutual smiles we did the same.

On the way out of the house, Mrs. Babin presented us with a huge sack loaded with sandwiches, vegetables, and fruit and insisted we eat all of it on the way to Lourdes since it was a fairly long distance away to the south.

As we proceeded south on a very fast train we met an Irish bishop leading his group of pilgrims to the Shrine of Our Lady of Lourdes. He mentioned that they were hungry and really couldn't afford the expensive meals in the dining car. I thought, "So that's why the Babin family gave sister and myself such a large lunch sack full of good food -- for all the bishop's friends!"

He accepted appreciably the whole thing and quickly distributed all the contents, all of which made us overjoyed once again at God's care for all his children.

THE MIRACLE OF OUR LADY
AT LOURDES

On August 14, 1984, after settling at one of the local hotels, we joined about 70,000 other visitors and pilgrims at the shrine of Lourdes. It was so beautiful! Sure enough there was the river nearby. I couldn't help wonder how Bernadette and her companions got over that river to collect wood for their poor stove. There must have been some kind of a bridge used to get over that stream, which was both wide and swift.

Sister Mary Frances remarked how she would so appreciate a miracle for her foot since the metatarsal bone had given her prolonged trouble and aches whenever she walked on it. I remarked, "Our Lord is the great healer, and Our Lady can intercede for us with her son, Jesus, just as she did at the marriage of Cana when she interceded with her Son and obtained a wonderful miracle of substantially changing the water into wine for the benefit of all."

We then proceeded over to the spring and then I had sister put her foot into the precious water. While I sprinkled water over her foot we prayed, "Father, you know all things. You know what is best for my dear friend, and we place our trust in your infinite love and wisdom. May we have a complete healing in Jesus' holy name and through the powerful intercession of Mary. We ask and thank you ahead of time. Amen." The next day I noticed that Sister Mary Frances was walking with much greater ease. She was so overjoyed, "No more pain!"

After dark the next evening on the feast of Our Lady's Assumption, thousands of us with our little candles processed around the shrine starting at the cove and proceeding in front of the big stone church with its many stairs and balcony. It was a sea of lights moving steadily while the rosary was said in a dozen languages.

At the beginning of the prayers and "Ave Maria," I was distracted by a beautiful globe of light gliding from the Easterly direction which stopped and placed itself right next to the church spires and stayed there for the entire rosary. I was thrilled to see what I believed was a real miracle—our blessed Lady visiting all of us, her spiritual children, given to her at the foot of the cross on Calvary almost 2000 years ago, and now blessing all of us. I wasn't the only one who saw it. There were many others around who also saw the glowing "globe" (for lack of a better description), and were pointing with joy-filled expressions. When the rosary was over the beautiful light moved back gently towards the east and then disappeared. I was thrilled and filled with so much joy at the privilege of witnessing our Lady's visitation on her big feast.

Sister Mary Frances saw it too, but had a different reaction, saying, "It's just a bright cloud."

"What!" I replied. "Since when does a cloud shine that brightly in one spot in the middle of the night long after the sun has disappeared. Besides that, since when does a cloud stay in one place by the spire for the length of a rosary and then go in reverse back towards the east again. Clouds don't come to a skidding halt and stay in one place for an hour, but would continue toward the west without stopping."

I'll never forget that special event. It fills my heart with so much awe and gratitude every time I think of it.

Sister De Sales had a different experience while at Lourdes. On the day she and thousands of others were at Benediction, many very sick people were brought forth on stretchers and small carriages drawn by dedicated volunteers. The sick were placed in many rows so the priest could carry the monstrance of the Blessed Sacrament along easily, making the sign of the cross in the blessing. There was a very ill man who looked like he had cancer and was near the end of his life lying on the stretcher next to sister.

She was very intent on Benediction and the proceedings among the other sick and the blessing of her section, when all of a sudden she was startled; the man beside her jumped up and yelled out, "I'm healed!" He ran towards the hospice building with the nurse trying to catch up with him. When she came back to the U.S.A. she related to us the miracle that she saw. Whether or not it was a miracle as investigated thoroughly by the church, we know it is proof that prayer is indeed answered, from the fact that hundreds of authenticated and documented cures have really taken place there and by the evidence of hundreds of crutches hanging by the cove, left by many healed people.

Next we traveled to Fatima, Portugal. We were very impressed by the faith of the people there. The pilgrims were slowly making their way to the shrine in groups of tens and twenties and at the last sixth of a mile many were seen sliding and shuffling on their knees along the cobbled stones toward the basilica doing penance and praying. What an example of unshakable devotion and love!

While there, staying with the Sisters of Perpetual Adoration, one of our hosts showed us several places many people don't know about.

One of the places was the small town of Santarem, a 45 minute ride south of Fatima. Our host took us to the church of St. Stephen of the Eucharistic Miracle. There were some parishioners making their holy hour in the church. Our guide, who had previous permission to open the tabernacle, beckoned Sister Frances and me to come to the altar where she placed the sacred monstrance. She held up a candle behind the exquisite glass pyx so we could see the Host that had visibly turned to flesh. We saw what looked like three strands of red blood trailing down to the bottom of the glass container where there was even more blood that had accumulated.

Later we learned that scientists had received the church's permission to take magnified pictures of the Holy Eucharist. It was found to be flesh of a human heart with blood type AB+. The same findings were authenticated at Lanciano, Italy, regarding the Holy Eucharist miracle that had taken place there.

The miracle that had taken place in Santarem took place in 1250 A.D. The story that was related to us centered around a poor woman who had many troubles, including marital problems, so much so, that instead of getting good advice from her pastor, or a good friend, the woman consulted a witch.

The witch said, "If your marriage is to improve, you must bring me a consecrated sacred Host." The poor woman went home and struggled with that demand. Finally after a serious battle with her conscience she finally consented to that act of sacrilege.

The next morning she put her scarf around her head and went to Mass. At the Communion time, she went up and received the Sacred Host and instead of consuming it, she took it out of her mouth and hid it in her scarf next to her face. After Mass as she was departing from the church, the Sacred Host started to bleed onto the floor with each step she took. Some of the parishioners noticed it and thought she was bleeding. They exclaimed their alarm and concern. This totally flustered the woman and she made some flimsy excuses and ran to her home.

She took the bleeding Host and placed it inside a large wood chest. That night she and her husband saw a strange light filling the room. It was coming from the chest! The wife broke down and cried, and told all that she had done that morning and how the witch had demanded the sacred Host be brought to her as a condition for improving her marriage.

The husband and wife made up and were reconciled. They knelt before the wood chest and the Sacred Host, and prayed throughout the night.

The next morning they mustered up courage to tell the whole story to the pastor. Upon hearing their account, he accompanied the couple back to their house. He carefully and reverently took the Sacred Host that had bled, back to the church, where he placed it into a beautiful wax box and put it into the church tabernacle.

The next morning the priest came to the church to say Mass. According to his custom he unlocked the tabernacle to check to see if there were enough consecrated Hosts for Mass or not. To his amazement, there, standing in the midst of broken wax pieces was a most exquisitely carved crystal pyx. Everyone who examined it thought that the angels formed it and brought it from heaven.

We will never forget that special incident of witnessing God's miracle of love and mercy.

After that profound experience, Sister and I started on our way to Paris via Lisbon and Irun. At the border between

Spain and France, we had a two hour wait. We had the unexpected joy of visiting a very old church where the relics of the saints Gerard Magellon and Gemma Galgani were kept.

Upon arrival in Paris we met a very friendly lady who came over to us and offered to take us to any place of cultural interest in Paris. We were delighted at her selflessness and her warmth. I said that we would be most grateful if she could ride with us in a taxi and explain about the gigantic structures of the Notre Dame Cathredral and the Tower. And she did! She was so patient and stayed with us until the right train came into the huge terminal. She motioned for us to get on the one with the blinking lights. We thanked her for her time and her loving care of two inexperienced travelers. She was, we concluded, an angel of the Lord in disguise, just like St. Raphael, who was such a good companion of Tobias, Jr., guarding and leading him.

It took many hours going through Belgium, then by boat over to Dover, England, and then once again on the train to Manchester, where the next day we would be flying home hungry and dirty. We hadn't a clue where to stay over night. We wanted a hotel that was close to the airport and one that could provide quick, free transportation to the airport. While we were mulling this over, a young smiling man carrying a brief-case got on the train and sat down next to us.

We got up our courage and asked him if he could tell us how to find a hotel in Manchester that would fit our needs, especially one near the airport. He opened his briefcase. It was totally empty except for a small book that listed all the area hotels.

He told us that this train would stop in two minutes and that we should get off then. We should not go into the city. Through the window he pointed to a hotel. "Take a taxi to that hotel." We thanked him, and raced toward the train's door.

Again, we believed that God had sent us an angel in disguise to help us when we needed it. Who else would have an empty briefcase with one book on local hotels? Angels are wonderful friends to have in our travels, not just here on earth, but also with us on the way to heaven and eternity.

THE NORTHERN LIGHTS AND PRAYER

During our first summer in Alaska, Rosella and I were commissioned by the bishop of northern Alaska to conduct student and adult religious education classes, to visit the Indian, Eskimo and white homes between the times of the actual classes and to lead in the liturgy on Sundays, whenever our missionary priest, Father Andrew Eordogh, S.J., couldn't make the trip from Holy Cross on the Yukon River to Aniak.

We were so pleased at our people's eagerness and openness to us. After visiting and giving religious instructions in the various villages as well as combating the "zillions" of mosquitos and no-see-ems, we were winding down, half dreading to leave for the southern "outside" states. We hated to say good-bye to our new found friends.

On the last evening about 11:30 p.m., before flying away, I remarked to Father Eordogh, as we were standing on the fifty-foot bank overlooking the Kuskaquim River, that I always wanted to see the northern lights first hand, but since it was summer, I assumed it would be impossible to see them.

Father Aordogh said to Rosella and myself that all things are possible through prayer. He then said, "Let's ask Jesus and Mary." We fervently said the Hail Mary with our Hungarian missionary and no sooner were we finished, when the whole sky was lit up by multitudes of moving, dancing ribbons of fantastic colors of blues, greens, reds and yellows racing back and forth in front of us. We were so thrilled to see the Lord's display of curtains of lights!

While we stood watching in utter amazement and joy, there was a great commotion among all the locals who were running out of their houses, scurrying to alert all their neighbors about the aurora borealis phenomena that never takes place in the summer, but only during the winter or at most late fall or early spring.

After watching for almost an hour we realized that the early morning flight would come all too soon and we wouldn't be ready to depart. So while slipping and sliding down the steep river bank towards the mission church, Rosella and I expressed our gratitude and thanksgiving to almighty God, who so graciously heard our prayers and answered in the "fast positive" manner. "Praise the Lord, for He takes such good care of small things as well as great things."

THE PINK LIGHT

It was a chilly, snow-threatening day in early December. The religious-ed. teachers were preparing to go home with their lesson plans, books and notes after a half day of a teacher training workshop. It was freezing with snowflakes accumulating on everyone's windshields. With whisk brooms and ice scrapers, all was in readiness. Some of the teachers begged me to stay overnight since it would be slippery, dangerous, and almost impossible to drive home safely. It had already turned dark. I thanked them for the offer of their hospitality but there was an important staff meeting back at home base the next morning.

The wind was blowing so hard on the straight-away proceeding down to Lake Crescent that the car was sliding off to one side of the road. By holding the steering wheel at an acute angle to the right, it held more or less to the right of the road. The snow by now was blowing almost horizontally, coming so fast and furious that my old windshield wipers had a difficult time keeping up with the deluge of flakes. I prayed to the Lord for His protection and that of Our Blessed Lady and His angels. "Please Lord, here's your beloved pest again. Please help me to get home safely. The lake is so long even when it's perfect weather. Thanks for hearing and answering."

By this time even after that fervent prayer I was really concerned. No car telephones existed at that time and my C. B. radio range was only five miles' radius at most, and I was miles from home. It was getting very late at night.

Quite quickly the road was thoroughly covered with the snow that hid the insidious ice. Where was the yellow line? With the powerful wind and snow blowing so hard obliterating everything in sight, I pictured my little car and myself landing upside down in the deep cold water of Lake Crescent. And it is indeed very deep. In one spot near Storm King Mountain they say it is 500 feet deep. An airplane that crashed in the lake years before has never been found. I told myself not to think so much and concentrate on the driving and praying. "Dear Lord, angels, please guide my old car."

And then it happened! As I was approaching a turn in the curvy road, I noticed what I thought was an oncoming car with soft glow lights made so by the multitude of snowflakes blowing. "Who in the world would be out here at this time of night in such a storm?" I steered the car to the questionable right side edge of the road, and went even slower as I drove around the curve. Having passed the curve, I exclaimed half aloud, "Where is this oncoming car? It's gone!"

Again, while approaching the next bend in the road, with a cliff half hanging over the curve, I witnessed the same soft pink light glowing from behind the cliff on the right. Again I expected a car coming towards me on the left. Again after passing that sharp curve where the light was coming from, there was no vehicle of any kind coming towards me at all. The "light" then dawned on me. The angels were guiding me with their pink light from around every dangerous curve. I could see so clearly with their help where every bend in the road was located and thus avoided a possible accident in a remote place where a person could easily freeze to death with hypothermia.

Between midnight and one o'clock an exhausted nun parked the car at the convent and came in on tiptoe so as not to wake everyone. I stopped by the chapel to give thanks for sending the angels to direct me safely home.

AN ANSWER TO PRAYER

I proceeded one foggy morning on Highway 101 South around the Hood Canal to Belfair to an energetic group of friends on an all day mini-retreat. While driving the car south along the usual glassy water soaked road, it became hazardous. Without a doubt it was one of the most unusual driving experiences of my life. Along the picturesque road to Belfair, a thick thick fog so dense, high and wide came along that I was forced to slow my little car down to almost ten miles an hour, just crawling along, straining and peering into the "soup" as pilots nicknamed it in aviation.

As I glanced at my watch, I thought to myself, "There was more than enough time scheduled to travel around the end of the Hood Canal to Belfair, but at this speed it was clear that the arrival will be delayed by as much as two hours, leaving our retreatants in the lurch."

I turned desperately to the Lord, who I remembered was

the Lord who walked on the water, stilled the storm, parted the sea, multiplied the food and provided water.

"Please, Lord, You are our Creator, nothing is too difficult for you. Take pity on our retreatants who will have to wait or who will leave to go home not being "fed". Lord, please send your angels to make a tunnel in that 99% impenetrable "wall", so I can arrive on time. Thanks for hearing my prayer."

As I was proceeding ever so cautiously around a bend, there was an honest to goodness tunnel waiting for me to traverse. "Thanks, Lord. Thanks dear angels, especially you, Saint Raphael!"

As I traveled, the tunnel was very much in evidence ahead of the car. I was able to go at top legal speed all the way. Almost speeding too fast in a few spots on the straight away, but believe it or not, when I glanced through the rear view mirror the tunnel collapsed and closed down behind the car, making the visibility nil once again, where I had just been. I was thrilled and grateful as I drove into the yard of our hosts where many cars were already parked. After turning off the engine and grabbing the posters, books and notes, I hurried into the house just as the clock showed 9:30. Whew! Just in time!

As the experience was joyfully shared, everyone rejoiced and praised the Lord for hearing fervent prayer and for making tunnels.

An interesting sequel took place on the way back to my home. The fog had fairly well dissipated. Once again, my beautiful angel gently but firmly warned, "Slow down and turn your up-beams on." No sooner had I obeyed when a half dozen does and one buck crossed the road. They were as startled as the driver was. I came within just a few inches from the last deer's tail. The up-beams gave a few extra split seconds in which to react. Once again, prayers of thanks were in order.

WHEN GOD SAYS NO TO OUR PRAYER

All of us have often heard that God loves us even if He has to say "no". He, in His perfect 20/20 vision, also gives us what we need even at the last minute, not necessarily what we think we want. Sometimes God answers our prayer so quickly for our sake with a yes; but I believe, more for the sake of the Lord's friends, those people who are listening to the truths expounded by the Lord and by the Church, and hopefully are trying to carry out those truths in daily Christian living.

I was in the village of Kotlik, Alaska. Late at night, an Eskimo lady rushed over to the place where I was studying and asked me to come and pray with her for her grandfather who was very ill. We prayed together and asked God to heal him, and to give him peace.

The next morning she came over and said that he had died with peace in his heart.

After Communion, I prayed, "Dear Lord, I prayed that this man would get well and he died. What a disappointment! How come?"

This was when I first got started in the healing ministry and praying with people. In my heart, the Lord took pity, and said, "I heard your prayer. I healed him by taking him home to heaven in peace."

Isn't that the best healing?

Sometimes God says no to our way of thinking.

"AND THE ANGELS WILL BEAR YOU UP"

Written by Sister Margaret

(The following is an account of a true incident which occurred on the remote Olympic Peninsula at a mission where the sisters have been involved in education and pastoral ministry for many years.)

"What 'fool' would make a U-turn in such a hazardous spot?" I asked myself in shocked disbelief. "And at approximately fifty miles an hour?"

Such questions flashed instantaneously through my mind as we rounded a curve at the legal speed of forty miles an hour. Within seconds the oncoming car crossed several lanes crashing into a guard rail. I knew that this was no intended U-turn, but a car out of control which rapidly fish-tailed from the guard rail hurling the small red car with its helpless and bloodied driver facing directly into the path of our eastbound car.

Bracing myself for a violent crash when our large, heavy car would crush the little one, I instinctively raised my hand to shield my face, moaning, "Oh, God!" as I did so. Instead of the tremendous shock I had expected, our car just shuddered to a halt upon impact with a slight jolt which caused my shoulders to move forward a mere couple of inches. The driver, Sister Mary Matthew, with tremendous control, had in a split second steered our car slightly to the right thereby avoiding greater damage and at the same time preventing our car from going into a tailspin.

In a flash, my companion wrestled open her jammed door and jumped out of the car. Her sole impulse was to bring solace to the bleeding, badly shaken-up girl in the red car. Not knowing the extent of her injuries, Sister led the girl in prayer, an Act of Contrition, and consoled her as best she could.

Providentially close at hand, an aid car responded quickly to our emergency summons. Within seconds of their arrival, careful hands had put a collar around the young girl's neck. Others blow-torched the door, jammed tight in the collision with the heavier green car. With blood dripping from a head wound sustained when she hit her head against the rearview mirror, the young traffic victim was gently transferred to a stretcher and within minutes the waiting ambulance sped her quickly to the Port Angeles Hospital three miles away.

During the inevitable questioning following an accident,

the young officer asked the routine question, "Were you wearing your seat belt?" Although not required by law in our state at that time, we answered rather guiltily that we had not. Sister Matthew then spoke up saying, "Our angels held us back." To which the officer didn't bat an eyelash, but proceeded with the remainder of the questions. Later we were to learn how correct she was!

With the questions finished and the debris cleared away, we were free to leave. Upon returning to the car we noted that the accident had flung our large Bibles far up under the dashboard. But together, Sister Mary Matthew and I affirmed that our jolt had been very slight causing only a forward movement of just a few inches at the time of impact. Both passenger doors, however, were difficult to open and close. Later we were to learn that in actuality, despite its strong structure, our car had been totaled, so radically had the collision turned it on its chassis.

Our late arrival at the healing ministry session called for detailed explanations. After coffee and some healing prayers, the leader, Art H. told us that he had stopped the group session at 10:10 a.m.. To the members he said quietly, "Let's stop. I see angels surrounding the sisters. I think they need our prayers." Fervent prayers were then directed to Almighty God asking Him to protect us.

Miles away at precisely 10:10 a.m. on a beautiful, clear, sunshiny November day, God had indeed protected all three of us as the green and the red cars collided on the curving road by Morse Creek. It was just at that time that an apparent "fool" had made an apparent U-turn endangering our lives. Inspection of the badly damaged red car later revealed that a blown tire had apparently caused the driver to lose control of her vehicle. That blew my theory about a "fool" making a U-turn on a curve at high speed. The fact was that the tires on the car were new. What had gone wrong?

Instead, it turned out that the driver was a beautiful young girl with a good driving record. Her grandmother was the secretary for the parish where we worked. While G's injuries were not too serious, the accident was an extremely traumatic experience. When informed that the healing ministry group had seen angels surrounding us at the time of the accident, G was profoundly moved and very grateful. Smiling wanly, she commented, "Well, if it had to be that I was to crash into someone, I'm glad it was you sisters and not some huge semitrailer truck." She was deeply appreciative of Sister Mary Matthew as her consoling "angel" immediately after the collision.

In an age when the belief in angels and their role in God's plan has been downplayed frequently, we felt that this was a striking reaffirmation of God's use of the angels to members of Queen of Angels Parish in a town named for the angels: Port Angeles.

GRABBED FROM HELL BY PRAYER

While visiting in a certain town, a desperate phone call came in the afternoon from a young lad. "Will you come to my friend's trailer, please! My pals won't listen to me. I tried to persuade them that playing around with the ouiji board, horoscopes, and palm reading is very dangerous. It's inviting the fallen angels and demons to come into our lives and do serious damage, trying to cause confusion."

I glanced at the calendar and sure enough, no meetings to attend or talks to give. I had no excuse not to make the short trip across town.

Over the phone, I gently tried to calm him down. "Don't be afraid or intimidated by the so-called "miracles" or manifestations of God's enemies. They are merely creatures. Ask the Lord in Jesus' holy name for protection, not only for yourself but also for every person, place or thing that is associated with you. We are winners with Jesus! Jesus said,

"Be of good courage, I have conquered the world." (John 16) Jesus meant that.

The boy felt a little better to learn that I could actually come that very evening. After hanging up I just stood there. "What to do and say? Lord, please enlighten me as to what to do and how. I surely need your help now."

On second thought, I remembered that the Lord sent the apostles and disciples out two by two to the various towns to evangelize, praying for people's needs. I remembered also what wonderful success they had, healing, delivering the supplicants from the power of the evil one. I called two of my friends who had gone through the healing ministry classes. With their promise to come with me to be prayer warriors and intercessors, I felt much more relieved that I would not be alone.

It was quite dark when the three of us arrived at the little trailer loaded with young people. After the welcoming, they shared the startling happenings regarding the ouiji board.

"It answered our questions and when we asked, "Who is God?" it said, "Satan, and when we asked, "Is Jesus God?" it furiously scribbled all over the paper incoherently."

After explaining that using the ouiji board can only bring forth evil fruit, we asked them to burn it. The next day after they agreed not to play around with it, they tried to burn it several times with no success, but finally, after invoking the powerful name of Jesus, it was burned totally. It was a real lesson for all of us. Once again it was brought home to us that we are indeed winners in Jesus' holy name.

Our young friend came for prayer off and on for five or six years. Quite a few problems were taken care of, thank God. We prayed, and his own family prayed for him. In praying with him on more than one occasion, we lovingly but firmly, among other things, stressed the importance of prayer, keeping the ten commandments, faithful attendance at Mass, receiving the sacraments, avoiding all persons, places or things that would take him from our God of love, to which he agreed. He sincerely tried to have a closer walk with Jesus.

For several years we lost track of him. We learned from the other members of his family that he got into questionable company with undesirable "friends," desiring acceptance. Looking for adventures, he became addicted to alcohol, drugs, girl friends, and having an easier life. As he got enmeshed in the so-called "good life," troubles flooded upon him: debts, borrowing, stealing. There were threats, arguments with his girl friend who wanted to abort their child, anxiety over saving his young son from being a possible victim of satanic ritual or abuse.

We prayed and his family prayed to almighty God, the saints, angels, and especially to our mutual friend, Padre Pio.

After several years of anxieties and unhappiness, a very eventful night would turn his life upside down and around. He went to see his girlfriend and their son. He noticed a real strain on the faces of those in the room, and so decided to leave. One of the guys offered to transport him back to town. Once on the road, that fellow driving the truck said calmly as he brought out his knife, "I hate to do this... but..." and started to stab him repeatedly. There were between 60 and 100 stab wounds. The blood spurted all over. Our young friend tried to defend himself by trying to dive out of the truck, crying for help... anyone's help. Beside the road, losing consciousness, he said later that he thought he was dying. He saw and felt his spirit leaving his body. He was plunging down a long tunnel faster and faster, and it became darker and darker. He just knew that he was going to hell. "Oh, God, help me!"

All of a sudden he saw the figure of a monk standing in the dark tunnel who caught and held him, keeping him from falling further into what looked like a deep black hole. The next thing he knew he was back into his body, still being held by this mysterious monk.

As he was being transported to the hospital he lost consciousness for his blood vessels had collapsed. His family, Sister Mary Frances, and I were called to come to the hospital and pray for him.

Prayers can even fill collapsed blood vessels. Many blood transfusions were given by the attentive doctors restoring his stiffened veins and arteries. He was in intensive care for several weeks. All the stab wounds were healed quickly except for a half dozen around his neck.

Another miracle took place in the hospital. He was willing to forgive and pray for his would-be murderer, and also to be an enthusiastic witness to how good God was to him. It was only later that he was shown a holy card picture of

Padre Pio, a Capuchin monk who had lived in Italy and died in 1968, many years previous to this event. He said excitedly, "That's the monk! He helped save me from hell!"

AN ANGEL WHO HAD THE POWER TO MAKE THINGS DISAPPEAR

One particular school year there was a change of personnel on the parish council where I worked as a religious education coordinator, and a new treasurer took over. He was a very conscientious, hard working person who wanted to do everything just right.

So in March at the parish council meeting all the leaders and representatives of the various parish organizations met and presented their annual working budgets. He looked at all the papers presented and announced that all the expenditures were too general. They all had to be made more detailed.

As a result, all of us representatives had to redo all the budgets. This never had happened before. The pastor had always been pleased with the various groups' frugalities, being careful to work in the "black." This went on month after month, the same dissatisfaction expressed by the new parish treasurer. All of us were getting exasperated with the many delays and extra work entailed in redoing the budgets again and again.

One warm day in June, the evening of the last parish council meeting for the closing of the school year, I had to go over to the parish office. After picking up some items, I just sat in the car more or less exhausted and frustrated at the many delays. I muttered to the Lord, "Dear Lord Jesus, I'm getting very disgusted! My school office and the programs are shutting down for the summer and I have to leave for Spokane soon. Would you please send my beloved angels, anyone will do, to make our parish council treasurer lose all his papers pertaining to the budgets, make them all disappear. Thanks for hearing my little prayer."

Sure enough, shortly after, the treasurer came over to my car where I was sitting. He had a very quizzical look on his face. "Sister," he said, "the strangest thing happened. Of all my papers, all my budget notes have mysteriously disappeared this afternoon. I know I left them in the usual definite place—but they are gone."

I tried to be sympathetic but inside my mind I was so grateful to the ever faithful angel to arrange the loss of not any of the other papers and reports but just the yearly budget's folder located in that same desk area. Inside I rejoiced and whispered a very quiet, "Hurrah! Thanks Lord."

And, sure enough, the meeting went smoothly and quickly. All the parish organizations' budgets were passed without a hitch and everyone heaved a sigh of relief. Everything was finished in record time. After coffee and cookies we all breezed home relieved. I thanked my neat, caring angel for a job well done.

OUR ANGEL
by Juliet Hubbs

Majestically he fills a room,
    A Spirit wise and bold.
Yet gentle is this Angel's touch,
    A blend of young and old.

He comes to earth for all of us
    To help us understand.
His energy of gentle strength
    Brings balance to the land.

His essence brings the hope of peace
    To love, not just survive...
To touch a place within our soul
    That makes us feel alive!

He urges us to be aware
    To see things as they are
To open up our hearts and trust
    He is a guiding star.

"Be not afraid of who you are,"
   You'll hear his tender voice.
"You have a chance to live your dream,
   So make a conscious choice."

SAVED FROM THE ELECTRIC CHAIR

It happened in a small mission parish. The parishioners were a very prayerful group who prayed their way through "thick and thin." Nothing seemed to daunt them in the slightest.

Such a one was Pedro, who brought his beautiful wife, Maria, and their only child, Miguel, to this outstanding and spectacular valley surrounded by snow-capped mountains and green hills.

They were especially hard-working Christians who labored faithfully for a local farmer and then would come always to the mission church to attend Mass. They gradually made themselves known, appreciated and loved by all the other parishioners.

Several years later, their son, Miguel, who was by this time very much part of the high school scene began to be associated with a questionable group of youths from a nearby city who lived in the "fast lane," speeding, cruising, using drugs, the whole bit.

This really worried his parents who tried their best to really talk with him about life's goals and avoiding any person, place or thing that would take him away from Christ, but to no avail. Miguel would be good for a while and then gradually slip back into his dubious life style.

Then one day it happened! Miguel didn't come home. He had gone with some of his buddies motorcycle riding on the mountain trails. All went well until they were returning home. There in the twilight of the sun's last glow, a screech of wheels and brakes took place. In a flash, an instant, a life was snuffed out. Miguel's motorcycle was no match for the semi-truck that rounded the corner.

After identifying Miguel at the hospital, the town policeman had the heartrending task of giving the news of the death of their only child to Pedro and Maria, who had just come home from working long hours in the fields.

They couldn't believe it! They wept holding each other, sobbing loud cries. Miguel was their pride and joy. Their hopes and plans were centered on their son.

It all was traumatic for Pedro especially. He became discouraged, and so depressed that he ceased going to Mass and receiving the sacraments.

As he became more and more despondent, he began to even blame God saying, "Why, oh God! I thought You were a God of love, of mercy, protecting your own. Now, You are silent!"

His fellow parishioners tried to comfort him at the funeral and especially in the days and weeks that followed. His wife attempted to encourage him, but it was almost impossible to get him even to speak.

Everyone missed him at church. They told Maria that they would storm heaven and pray for a miracle for Pedro, and of course for her also.

Not long after, about a month later, even though it seemed like an eternity, Pedro received his miracle!

He and Maria appeared at church the next Sunday morning, all smiles. Their friends gathered around the happy couple after Mass. They exclaimed, "What happened? Tell us."

Pedro, very demonstratively said, "Last night, I went to bed early, completely exhausted. Looking back, I still don't know whether it was a vision or just a vivid dream. But my son, Miguel, appeared in light with his little dog at his side. He was radiantly happy. He said, "Dad, why do you grieve so for me? Please don't. God, in His infinite love and perfect wisdom saved me from the electric chair."

Miguel showed his dad four scenes of what would have happened if God in His mercy and love, hadn't taken him to heaven.

The first scene illustrated Miguel joining in with really evil company and getting into the horrible addictions of drugs and alcohol.

The second scene showed Miguel and his companions stealing to support their habits.

The third scene showed Miguel robbing a bank and killing a policeman.

The fourth and last scenario showed Miguel in an electric chair.

He continued, "Dad, this would have happened to me, if

God in His merciful love and wisdom, hadn't taken me then; as it is, I am so happy." He turned and disappeared into the brilliant light.

Pedro could hardly contain himself relating to everyone about the miracle of grace.

Everyone heaved a big sigh of relief, and gave thanks to God for having heard their collective prayer for the saving of a son, for the salvation and the healing of the precious family, and for giving peace to all.

OUR FRIENDS AND ANGELS
A True Happening with Prayer
by Rosa Achzinger, Port Angeles, Washington

Just a short note to say hello and to tell you of a tremendous religious encounter I experienced last July.

My husband and I were sound asleep when I was awakened by a silent voice (I say silent, because the voice was in my head, and I was the only one who could hear this voice). The voice said, "Listen." Mentally I asked, "Listen to what?" The voice just replied, "Shh, listen." I then sat up in bed real quiet. Seconds later I heard the sound of screeching tires, then a crash. I immediately woke my husband and said to him, "Daddy!" (I always call him Daddy). "There has been an accident." He woke up and said I was dreaming for this was happening at about 2:00 a.m.. I said, "No, I am not dreaming." He then arose out of bed, got dressed and went to see. Sure enough there was a small pickup upside down on our road, with a young man trapped inside. His legs were pinned under the dash board and he kept asking my husband to please help him. I called 911 and asked for an ambulance. The firemen used the "jaws of life" (a tool to cut the auto) to free the young man.

While this is happening, this voice kept urging me to pray, so I started to say the rosary. Usually I only say an Our Father and a couple of Hail Mary's but this voice was insistent on my saying more than just a few prayers. I just had finished saying the rosary and my husband walked in.

One or two days later a woman came to our home. She was the mother of the young man. She wanted to thank my husband for helping her son. I asked how her son was doing and she said he was home. The hospital released him with a few bruises. He was shook up but he was fine. To me, this is a miracle. His guardian angel was watching over him. There's no doubt in my mind about that. The woman was amazed and in awe.

I believe that his guardian angel, or mine, was the one that woke me up and spoke to me, because the young man was not listening.

MARIAN HALVORSON'S STORY

I was in Ipoh, Malaysia, during Easter 1978 while on an Asian safari for Intermedia (N.C.C.A.). That Lenten-Easter weekend there were special evangelistic healing services at two Chinese speaking churches. The bishop of the Malaysian church, Dr. Peter Foung, was there together with two American pastors from Mjorud's Evangelism Association, Reverend Art Mueller and Reverend Jim Roberson.

After the Good Friday message, people streamed to the altar: some Buddhists to receive Jesus, others to be prayed over for healing, and others to experience anew the power of the Holy Spirit for ministry. As I sat there in prayer with them, a young Chinese man came up to me and asked, "Are you a Christian?"

"Yes," I replied, "I've been in the Lord's work in Africa for the last 30 years."

"And, do you believe Jesus heals today?"

"Yes, I've experienced His healing and I know He heals today."

"Good!" he continued. Then he stretched out his arm and asked, "You see this arm?" It looked perfectly normal and then he continued, "Last year I was a Buddhist, and I'd had polio as a small child and this arm came only to the elbow with five little fingers right here." He pointed to his elbow.

"A friend of mine invited me to these services, so I came with him. That night when people went to be prayed for, I saw a little old lady whom I knew was a staunch Buddhist crawl up to the altar. She was very deformed and her back looked like the letter "S." As she received Jesus and was prayed for, those around her started to clap their hands, but I was sitting way in back so I couldn't see what had happened. The next night I had to go back again and there was that lady walking like a young lady with her back straight and healed! I could hardly wait for the call to prayer that night. After I accepted Jesus, the American evangelist (Dr. H.J. Mjorud) and our bishop asked if I wanted prayer for healing. As they prayed, my arm grew out instantaneously with all these fingers in their right place!"

Marveling, I asked, "And what is your name?"

"I was baptized Derek, because I learned that a derrick is a machine which carries stones to make walls for buildings. I want to be someone who helps Jesus take dead Buddhist stones and place them in the temple of the living God!"

"And what are you doing these days?"

"I'm selling Christian books in the market. But I'm waiting for the doors to open into China, so I can go there and witness to my own people about Jesus."

Yes, it is time we take a fresh look at what God is doing here in our land and around the world.

FIRE AND THE POWER OF PRAYER
by Kathy Moore. Etna, California

On Friday, November 17, 1995, I spent the day in prayer for two friends in the hospital. In the afternoon about 2:00 I raked leaves for a little while and then my neighbor said to me from over the fence that he was planting 3000 redwood trees. This was the first time he had ever spoken to me.

I raked and I thought. I keep envisioning fruit trees and roses every time I look at one of my fields. This is ridiculous because fruit trees don't do that well here in the valley, roses are a favorite delicacy for the deer, and I want to keep that field clear in hopes of having a horse again someday. Yet when I look at the field, I see fruit trees and roses. I am not an imaginative person, so this was very weird to me. I cannot even explain what I mean when I say I see this, for I don't really. I just can't explain it.

Well, I was thinking of all this and prayed, "Lord, is this

vision from you? Do you really want me to plant these things?"

I got no answer, but after a while I went over to the neighbor and asked if he had ever done this before, plant trees. He said no. He just had this impulse to plant 3000 redwood trees. His wife said she thought the idea utterly ridiculous.

I said, "I was thinking I should plant my field with fruit trees. Do you think I should burn it first?"

He didn't answer whether or not I should burn it, just that if I did, I shouldn't worry about it getting away at his side of my property for there was nothing to burn. Also on my side, with my lawn, it wouldn't spread. But another neighbor's field to the west of mine was all tinder dry tall grass. It was mid-November and we had not yet had any winter rains. The wind usually came from the west so my neighbor suggested that I should start at the west end of my field. He suggested now was a good time to do it because it was going to rain in three days. He said days, but maybe he meant hours. And I took his "now" to mean, "right now".

It was 3:30 p.m.. I got a broom, shovel and hose ready and set the grass on fire at the northwest side. A grass fire only burns at the perimeter and spreads out at its edges as it burns. This fire started off slowly toward the east. As it began to spread out, I heard, high overhead, a sound I thought was a huge jet flying over head. It wasn't a jet. It was the wind.

Suddenly the wind swooped down and with one mighty gust whipped the fire to the west, into my neighbor's field.

There it roared, four feet high, and straight toward an open hay barn.

I scrambled over the fence where a bear had knocked it down. I tripped and fell and as I rolled up I prayed, "Lord, help me!"

The prayer no sooner left my lips when the wind immediately died and with a few slaps of my broom the fire was out.

I climbed back into my field and continued to burn a small triangle, the wind barely blowing it to the east. That took about a half hour before the fire went out.

I then lit another section of the field, again starting on the west side. This time I quickly beat it out along side the fence so it wouldn't back-burn. The fire burned slowly, very slowly toward the east. I began to think that I was awfully stupid to be burning this field alone. I should have waited until a day when my son was home. I also thought it was beginning to spread out too far, I ought to start beating out the edges, and this was going to take days to burn if I had to keep beating it out, when again, I heard this sound of a jet coming from high in the sky. I knew now that it was no jet.

Now that I had experienced no control over a grass fire once the wind hit it, I was scared stiff and prayed, "God, help me with this fire."

With a swoop the wind grabbed that fire and drove it eastward. The blaze soared four feet high. There was absolutely no way I could have stopped it. It burned east and a little north until it came near the edge of the field, then the wind turned and blew south and drove the fire in a straight line. When the fire was four feet from the south fence, it turned and blew the fire west until it was about six feet from the west fence. Then the wind died. The field was burned.

The moment that fire turned for the third time and headed west I knew I was witnessing an awesome sight. I knew I was witnessing the power of God within that fire and wind. And I was nothing compared to it.

With the wind gone, the fire burned slowly, a tiny line four feet from the south fence and six feet from the west fence.

I drew an imaginary line two feet from the south fence and thought, "When the fire reaches there I'll beat it out with the broom," and prayed, "Please don't let the wind catch it and blow it past that two feet."

When the fire hit this imaginary line, which still had in it leaves and grass, it went out. Poof!

I only had the far southwest corner to burn. There were about twelve little spot fires burning in that corner, plus there was a big fire in the middle of the field where a pile of sticks were burning. I was just thinking of putting out these little fires, when poof, they all went out at once, even the large fire in the center. They went out as if a candle snuffer had dropped down upon them.

I stood there, and said, "Lord, what about all these little sparks lying here and there amongst the leaves? A wind could fan them into flames during the night."

I no sooner thought this when it started to rain, just like

that. It continued to rain all night and continued for several days. Everything turned sopping wet. My field would have been impossible to burn.

To witness such a miracle of wind and fire was absolutely awesome! To realize my lack of control, my littleness and God's greatness manifested before me is mind boggling.

I was in the house before 5:30 with my field burned in a nice square way.

Eternal Father, we sing a song of hope. Hope that indeed, You are with us and are holding us in Your hands.

ON A MOUNTAIN PASS
by Sister Sioban

When I was a little girl, my mother told me this story, so it could have happened over 100 years ago.

A young man was drafted into the army, and one day his officer said to him, "I'm going to send you on a very dangerous mission. This sealed envelope has a very important message inside, so get your horse. You must go over this mountain pass and across the enemy line. There's a great possibility you'll never make it. If you make it, you go to a certain number, and deliver this envelope. The man is one of my spies and he'll give you an envelope to bring back to me. Good luck, God speed." And the soldier went away on horseback.

Well, it was near dusk that evening. He was riding straight ahead and all at once a very beautiful lady came forward. She was holding a lantern and she took hold of the reins and she led the horse to the left. She patted the horse on the neck and she gave a sign, "Go this way."

The young man went on and he crossed the enemy lines and was not seen by the enemy. He got to the house where he was supposed to go and met the man he was supposed to meet and gave him the envelope. The man gave him a meal and said, "Now you best be on your way."

He got a couple of hours of rest and he started out very early in the morning. He reached the pass where he had met the beautiful lady the night before. He thought, "Now that it's bright, I hope I get to see this lady. I can see her lodge (very likely she's living there in a lodge and she's paid to help people in the pass)."

He came along, but there was no sign of a lodge, no sign of the lady. He couldn't understand. After a couple of weeks, he forgot about it, and when the war was over he returned home.

He had been raised by his grandmother, so when he arrived at the house, she kept him up half the night asking him all kinds of questions about what happened. He said to her, "Oh, I must tell you something about the time my officer sent me over the mountain pass on a very dangerous mission."

He told her all about this beautiful woman and how he could not find her lodge and he never found her. The grandmother looked at him and she said, "If you could see a picture of her, would you recognize her?"

He said, "Oh, yes, of course, I would. I'll never forget her face."

The grandmother went upstairs to the loft and opened an old trunk and brought down a picture and said, "Is this the lady you saw?"

"Oh yes! That's the very lady! Do you know her?

She said, "Yes, that is my daughter, your mother. She died the night that you were born. When you were drafted, I prayed to her several times a day. I asked her with confidence for I knew she went to heaven, "Please watch over James and bring him back safe and sound." So she answered my prayer."

The young man was delighted to find out who his mother was and that he had actually seen her on the mountain pass.

ABOUT PRAYER
by Sister Sioban

I'll tell you another story about prayer. When I was 14 years old I used to attend many of the adult missions. This one particular night I went to the special mission given by two Redemptorist fathers which was all about prayer, one of my favorite subjects.

The Redemptorist fathers said that way back, a young girl, who was born in Tralee, was raised by an aunt, since her parents had died. She went on and trained to be a nurse and then the aunt died. She had no one depending on her so she went to London, England. She did very well and she lived in a flat with another nurse. They were good friends, and the other nurse had alot of friends in London, so she took Mary with her when she was invited out to parties.

This one night Mary met a very handsome man at the party and he began to date her. Well, after a few months she discovered he wasn't a Catholic, so she said to him, "I'm very sorry, but I'm a Catholic and I go to church every morning, and I would have no business marrying a man who's not a Catholic."

He made all kinds of promises. He said, "Your religion is yours. I have mine. I'll never bother you. You can go to church any time you want. It makes no difference to me."

So he kept on coaxing her to marry him. She had a lot of doubts about it, but eventually she married him.

The Sunday after they were married, she was in her room fixing up her hair and he walked in and he said, "Where in the world are you going?"

She said, "I'm going to Mass."

"Oh, forget all that rubbish," he said. "You're not going to any Mass. You're coming to my church with me."

She said, "Oh, no, I cannot do that."

He said, "Of course you can."

So she walked out the door and went to church, the Catholic church, and of course the Mass and the sermon, everything was so long, that he was out of his church long before she was, so he was home first. When she got into the house, she discovered that the beautiful statue of the Virgin Mary that her aunt had given her when she was going to London was broken in smithereens. She never said a word. She picked up all the pieces and put them in the garbage.

In the meantime, she bought a picture of Our Lady of Perpetual Help and the following Sunday when she got home from church, he had dug his heel right into the face of the Virgin Mary.

So she said nothing, and pretended that she never even noticed, picked up the picture and put it into the garbage can. Then she went shopping the next day and bought an exercise book and with a ruler and a pen she margined it off and she wrote on top, "Mass and Holy Communion for the Conversion of my Husband."

In the next margin she put down, "Rosary." Then she put down, "Ejaculations," how many ejaculations she said, and the day, which went up into the hundreds. On the outside margin of the page, she wrote, "My husband called me, "Catholic fool" today but I never said a word. I never answered him. I offered it up for his conversion." That went on for about three years.

One night she developed a most awful pain in her side. She didn't say anything. Her husband was a lawyer. He went off to his office and she told the servant. The servant said, "Oh, ma'am, we best call a doctor."

She said, "Oh, no. This pain is really, really bad. I know I'm not going to survive. So don't say anything to my husband until I'm dead, then call his office."

So she sat on the chair and she was bent over with the pain and the poor servant was in agony. She wanted to help her but didn't know what to do. Her mistress wouldn't let her call the doctor. After a few hours, she passed away.

The servant called the husband and he came home, and he was all in a dither. The servant said to him, "You know, sir, you have to make contact with the parish priest because she was a Catholic and you have to arrange for the Mass, the funeral and all that."

So he went down to the rectory and made arrangements for the Mass and he was such a bitter Protestant, he would not even go into church for the Mass. He waited outside until they brought the coffin out. He did go to the cemetery.

His mother then joined him. She began going through his wife's clothing and her jewelry. He went into her room and the first thing he spotted was a string of rosary beads. He grabbed them and threw them across the room and said, "Some more of that Catholic trash." Then he began going through the jewelry and giving pieces to his mother. Then he spotted this exercise book. He took it out into his office and began reading the pages. He saw all the times he called her names and how she never said a word and offered it up for his conversion. He only got halfway through the book when he felt a very soft feeling going through his heart. He felt like crying for the first time he could ever remember.

There was a life size picture of herself over her bed. He looked up at her picture and said, "Mary, you have won." He closed the exercise book. He went down to the rectory and the housekeeper opened the door when he rang the bell. The housekeeper thought, "Oh, my goodness, me, that awful man is here." So she went up to the parish priest and said, "Oh, Father, you'll never believe it, that Mr. So and So is downstairs to see you. What would he ever want?"

He said, "I don't know, child, but I'm sure going to find out." So he came down and he put his glasses down on his nose, and said, "Yes, Sir, what can I do for you?"

The man stood up and said, "Father, I want to be a priest."

"Oh, oh," the parish priest said, "that takes a long time.

You've got to start by taking instructions. You've got to be baptized a Catholic. There's a lot of steps to it, and then you get to the seminary."

"Well," he said, "that's all right. I'm going to do all those steps you're talking about, but I don't want to be a priest like you. You know, this is an easy life what you have right here. I want to go to Africa and work with the natives."

So the parish priest got him started on instructions and he went ahead. He was ordained and he said his first Mass right there in the parish where his wife had died. Nobody knew who he was, because he was never around the Catholics. He told the whole story of the conversion of this certain man and when he finished he looked at the congregation and said with great emotion, "That priest is me, right here." The whole congregation broke into tears. Afterwards he did go to Africa.

As I said in the beginning, I was just 14 years old when the Redemptorist priest told us that story. He said, "That priest is still working in Africa and I know him. He is a marvelous priest."

So you see what a wonderful change came into his life because of the prayers and sacrifices that his wife made. It was a hopeless situation, but she did the right thing.

INNER LOCUTIONS BY MY GUARDIAN ANGEL
by Carol L. Stromberg

In the year, 1959, I received the miracle of the gift of faith and was received into the Catholic church. At the time of my conversion, I was carrying my third child in my womb.

After my baptism, I joined the choir and loved the Gregorian chant. I enjoyed spiritual reading, especially the works of Thomas Merton, and worked in the parish library. I was soon invited to be library chairman for our local guild at St. Joseph the Worker Church in Canoga Park, California.

One evening, I was attending a guild meeting and I arrived late. The home was located in a cul-de-sac. I had to park further away down the street.

After the meeting, as I walked to my car, one of the members offered to give me a ride. I thanked her, but walked down the unlit street. As I closed my door, I heard an interior voice command, "Push your car lock down." I obeyed and immediately there was the face of a man lunging at me, directly at my windshield. He appeared to be drunk and staggered all around my car.

I knew I was safe, but the element of surprise frightened me. The engine of my Ford station wagon had a tendency to stall. Sure enough, it stalled three times before I could turn around. I could see the man's face before me, so I lost myself quickly in a maze of traffic. When I arrived home, I related the experience to my husband. He said, "There was a report of a rapist in the area." I thanked God for the timely inner voice of my guardian angel for protecting me and the unborn child in my womb.

In the following year, my husband, a model railroad buff, decided to take the last ride on the Pacific Electric Street car from Los Angeles to Lynwood, California. He invited a friend and we drove to Exhibition Park to allow me and my baby daughter to have a visit to the art museum. We made an agreement to meet at the entrance at closing time. The exhibit of Egyptian artifacts were on display, to my delight!

After a while I rested on a bench and fed my infant daughter, Lorraine. An interior voice spoke a command for the second time, "Get up, cross the room, go to the next room."

As I obeyed, I could hear a loud crashing noise behind me. Apparently, support for the display case was somehow weakened and broken and a wall of glass crashed to the floor behind the place where I had been sitting.

When it was closing time, I waited for my husband to pick us up. After an hour or so, a lady from the apartment building across the street saw me pushing the baby stroller. She was kind enough to come and offer the use of her telephone, saying, "I don't even empty my garbage after dark in this neighborhood." I felt protected and thanked her, saying my husband would arrive soon.

Another couple saw my plight as my baby daughter dropped her glass bottle, breaking it on the pavement. I declined their offer of help, having faith that I would somehow be protected. My husband finally arrived. He said, "It took a lot longer to make the trip than I realized."

These experiences have increased my awareness of the spiritual realm surrounding us, and the protection and the loving care of God. And I thank Him daily for our angelic beings, our friends.

MY CHILDREN AND I ARE ALIVE! PRAYER WORKS

by Margaret Fay Vines

My husband, Ariel, and I were married in 1946. Ariel was a good, hard working man who faithfully read the Bible. After 22 years of marriage, he converted to the Roman Catholic faith. We had ten children, six sons, and three daughters, and one son who died as an infant.

When our first born son, Gerald, was a teenager, he was helping his father with some carpenter work. While he was bent over using the saw, he backed up against the kitchen door which had glass in it. The glass shattered and a spear of glass went through him. We rushed him to the hospital. He was bleeding profusely. The nurse could not find any pulse and rushed him into the emergency. I believe it was through the many prayers offered up and through the grace of God that he lived. Prayer works!

I almost lost my fifth child, John. When I was six months along with him, my water broke and I went into labor. My doctor met me at the hospital and informed me that the baby would arrive by evening but would not live. I told him I would not deliver if he would not live. I got out my rosary and proceeded to pray.

The doctor came back to check on me each evening, and each morning was very sure I was going to deliver that day. He kept saying that I would lose my baby. This continued for several days. He finally sent me home with orders to go to bed.

I had three small children and a working husband. I rested as much as I could and took care of the children. I carried John full term. God had plans for him for he was ordained a priest in 1998.

I almost lost my next son, Daniel, when he was a teenager. Dan went hunting with his brothers, Ray and John, and his brother-in-law, Steve. While Ray and Steve were in a store, John and Dan started to fool around with the gun, pulling the trigger as they pointed it at each other. Suddenly a bullet that was lodged in the barrel went off, blowing the calf of Dan's leg off. Dan was rushed to the children's orthopedic hospital. Through the grace of God, the good doctors were able to save Dan's life and his leg.

Dan had another near death experience when he and John were in a car accident. Dan received a broken neck. The doctors said he should have died, and it was a miracle that he lived.

Our second daughter, Margaret Ann, is very strong in her Christian beliefs. When a man on T.V. said, "A woman with a collapsed lung is being healed. Repeat this prayer," Margaret said the prayer with me, and my lung became un-collapsed.

Through the power of prayer, my children and I are alive today. I give God thanks for watching over all of us.

CAR OUT OF CONTROL
by Susi Pullen. Homer, Alaska.

One winter day in Alaska I was driving up an icy hill that had on one side a very steep cliff—about 1000 feet straight down. I had in my car my mother, six-year-old daughter and four-year-old nephew. All was going well until I got to the top of the hill. Suddenly the car began to fish tail - the rear end began to swerve back and forth. I panicked and tried to control the car with steering and brakes. We were headed straight for the cliff. Suddenly I heard a calm male voice say, "Put in the clutch." As soon as I did, the power to the motor was cut and I gained control of the car. We stopped within one foot of going over the cliff. I prayed in thanksgiving for the rest of that day.

SAVED BY MY GUARDIAN ANGEL
by Rebecca Duncan. Shoreline, Washington

In the fall of 1984 I lived in Bremerton, Washington, with my husband and two small sons.

My friend, Maryanne, lived in Silverdale, another small town about ten miles from where I lived, with her husband and four young children. Her husband was the coach of a high school football team.

On this particular day, Maryanne called and asked if I would like to go with her that night to one of her husband's games. He would be going on the bus with the team and so she would be driving alone if I did not go with her.

The moment she asked if I would go with her, I heard a very clear voice in my head say, "No! Do not go!" For some reason I knew it was the voice of my angel. I did not tell Maryanne what I heard, but the voice repeated, "Do not go!" As we continued speaking on the phone, I sensed that there was a great danger if I went with her to the game, but feeling badly that if I did not go with her she would have no one to go with, I accepted.

After we got off the phone, the voice continued off and

on throughout the day, "Do not go!" It was as clear as someone standing right next to me and had the tone of a great warning of danger. You would think if I had any sense at all I would obey that voice!

I was very afraid of what it meant, but I foolishly drove to her house to pick her up that night. We had about a fifty mile distance to drive.

I did not want to concern her with the warnings I had been receiving all day, but finally, before we left her house, I decided I should say something. I simply told her that I had a kind of bad feeling about our trip that night. She looked at me and said that she, too, had some sort of uneasy feeling about it, and so we prayed together for God's protection over us before we drove off. Thank God we did that!

It was a chilly evening, but the football game went well. Still, all evening I kept thinking to myself, so far so good... fully aware that at any moment something awful was supposed to happen. I had a feeling of dread, but as a consolation I kept reminding myself that we had prayed for protection. "Dear God, please be with us and send Your angels to keep watch over us."

After the game it was getting late and we were hungry, so on the way home we stopped in a small out of the way restaurant for a bite to eat. "Still, so far, so good," I thought.

We had about thirty miles to go until we were safe at home and out of danger. About midnight I was beginning to feel a sense of relief because there wasn't much farther to go. Perhaps we had somehow bypassed the danger.

At one o'clock in the morning we were only two miles from the exit off the freeway to Maryanne's house. I was in the far left lane of the freeway. At this point I was thinking of moving over to the right lane for my exit, but had not yet done so. There were very few cars out at that hour of the night.

There were a number of curves in that stretch of freeway, and as we rounded one of the curves I glanced at Maryanne briefly as we chatted. Just at that moment she screamed, "Watch out!"

I immediately turned to see two big round head-lights coming right at us approximately ten feet in front of us! In that split second I knew with utter certainty that we were dead and that there was nothing I could do to avoid a head on collision. Even so, I turned the wheel hard right so at least I could say I'd made some effort, knowing full well there was absolutely no point in doing so. This all happened, of course, in a split second. In that very instant, in the blink of an eye, the car, with us in it, was sitting three lanes over on the right shoulder of the freeway, pointing straight ahead, sitting perfectly still with us and the car completely untouched and unharmed. My angel had placed us and the car over there . . . just like that! It happened so fast we didn't see it happen.

The reality of what had just happened put me in a state of utter shock. We were supposed to be dead and yet we were definitely still alive! I glanced around in disbelief and then turned around to see where the other car was. It was continuing down the wrong side of the freeway as if nothing had happened. I offered a brief prayer for the safety of that driver and any other people whom the driver might endanger that night.

Then I turned to Maryanne and screamed, "My angel saved us! My angel saved us!" She said, "God wanted us alive for a reason... some mysterious reason."

I personally thanked God for saving us, even though I disobeyed His messenger, my dear precious angel, who warned me so clearly not to go that night. How wrong I was to disobey.

I have thought of the miraculous incident thousands of times since that day and I am so humbled by it. I am deeply thankful for God's loving mercy because not only did my husband get to keep his wife, and my two young sons get to keep their mommy, but two years after the freeway miracle God gave us another miracle: a third son, who has been a great blessing in our lives. He would not be here today had it not been for God's loving providence in sending my angel to save my life. So I thank God for sparing our lives and I thank Him for teaching me a lesson in obedience and mercifully giving me another chance.

PRAYER AND BAPTISM SAVE A LIFE
by Tom Wiedt. Overland Park, Kansas

A young boy, about 15 years old, was playing with a shotgun. It went off and put a big hole in his left chest and shoulder. One of his friends ran across the street to get help. He found a neighbor and told him that his friend was seriously wounded.

The neighbor yelled to his wife to get some towels and water, and to meet him at the young boy's house. He saw how serious the wound was and put pressure on it to slow the bleeding. The boy was in terrific pain and the man knew it was a mortal wound. He knew that the boy was not baptized, so he proceeded to pour water on his head and baptized him. The boy stopped moving and went into a sleeping state. The emergency paramedics came and took him to the hospital, where he was in surgery for many hours.

The next day, the young boy's father came over to the

neighbor and told him that the boy wanted to see him right away, even though he was in intensive care. His son wanted to talk to him as soon as possible. The neighbor said he would wait for the boy to come home from the hospital, but the boy's father said that his son insisted that he come to the hospital now.

The neighbor went to the hospital. The young boy told him that when he started pouring the water on his head during the baptizing, all the pain from the shot-gun injury went away. At the same moment he saw angels standing behind the neighbor and floating above him during the baptizing. He then went to sleep and woke up in the hospital.

The boy fully recovered with no after effects from the injury.

PRAYER AND AN ANGEL
BRING A DRINK
by Pat Madauhs

One summer, while vacationing in a lovely resort in the Caribbean, I decided to take a walk to the nearest town. I set out around noon, without a hat or water, to just "follow the road." After walking about three miles, it began to dawn on me that this town was not close by, that it was probably farther than walking distance, and that the already hot sun was bearing down relentlessly without mercy.

I began feeling a little woozy from the heat, and began to realize that I had gotten myself into a dangerous pickle if I stayed out in the hot sun much longer. I began praying to God for sheer help.

The road was not heavily traveled. Only two cars had passed since I started walking. I was in trouble and there was no one to help me. I felt a little scared. "Please, Lord,"

I prayed, "I'm so thirsty. My body desperately needs water. Please help me."

A few steps further there was a bend in the dirt road, and another long stretch of road loomed before me. My heart sank. Just then, to my left, I saw a Caribbean native woman, in a brown dress and with a turban on her head, standing behind a wooden rail fence, beckoning to me to come over to her. Her expression was one almost of impatience, as if she had been standing there waiting for me and was wondering why I had taken so long to reach this spot in the road. In other words, her body language seemed to convey the message that she was tired of waiting for me! Or maybe she was disgusted at the dumbness of a person walking in the noonday sun, when the trees on either side of the road cast no shadows, without a hat for protection from the sun and without water.

In her two hands she carefully cradled what looked like a pear, some type of native fruit. She held it out for me to take, treating that fruit with great reverence and respect.

I took one look at the fruit and my thoughts shot to heaven. "The Lord heard and was answering my prayers." The woman looked at me with deep compassionate gravity in her eyes, as if to say, "Without this gift of God, you would suffer serious heat stroke. Learn your lesson and respect the sun from this day forward."

I took the fruit from her hands and thanked her with great sincerity and gratefulness. She abruptly turned her back to me and started walking away.

"This is exactly what I need!" I thought, as I enjoyed the first juicy bite. I never before had any juicy fruit that tasted so good! "Thank you, Lord! Thank you God for answering my prayer!"

I turned to catch a final glimpse of the very kind stranger lady, who had appeared out of nowhere, in the middle of a field, with no visible house, and I was quite surprised to see no one there. It seemed like the field was too large for her to have traversed it already. This was puzzling at the time. Now I know that angels disappear like that. I had eaten about half of the "pear" when a truck carrying a load of people headed for the town stopped and urged me to get on. They were dismayed to find me at that place on the road. The providence of God shone most clearly for me on that day.

UPON THIS ROCK
by Claudia J. Carabba

I was making a final trip to the church in Skull Creek Pass along the wintry, ice-laden river road through the majestic canyon. I wanted a memory imprint of every square inch of this journey. I wanted to remember the quaint charm of the weather-worn, turn of the century church, the glorious colors of the stained glass windows and the matching beauty of the weathered and weary faces I'd just left. For four years God had granted me a magnificent life here; the church folk, wilderness hikes, freshly caught trout suppers around the campfires, friends who had become family, healing outdoor mineral hot springs, wild west history, and a new-found interest in geology. I had also discovered a connection with the wilderness I never knew I possessed.

Pondering these thoughts, a movement caught my attention out of the corner of my eye. A small boulder, loosened from its frozen perch on the steep hillside by the heat of the rising afternoon temperatures, was tumbling erratically and rapidly down the hillside towards me. Time froze. My foot came off of the gas pedal as I looked at the oncoming lane for traffic and then behind for followers, thinking to myself that when I swerved to miss the boulder I would be hitting someone or be hit from behind.

Seeing no vehicles ahead or behind I glanced just in time to witness the boulder as it haphazardly bounded from the shoulder directly into the middle of my lane. It struck the road dead-center lifting the car's front end off the ground. The car began precariously lifting and turning onto its side, all of its wheels off of the ground, and began rolling over the bank. I peered out the window at the river below, which had somehow repositioned itself and was now directly in front of me. Thinking the river must be 40 to 50 feet down, I closed my eyes and wondered how long it would be before the imminent impact. I began silently praying the Lord's prayer. I felt suspended in time. Still. Motionless. "Why hadn't I hit the ground below?" I wondered.

I opened my eyes to find I was looking directly into the eyes of an incredibly beautiful and serene angelic being. There on each side of the car was an angel smiling at me. Together they effortlessly lifted my car and righted it, stopping the car from its perilous roll. They gently set the car down on the shoulder of the road. Never taking their eyes from me a calm reassurance pervaded my being and, with a gentle loving gesture of acknowledgment, as suddenly as they had appeared, they were gone.

I sat quietly, peacefully, for a moment completely enveloped in a loving calm. I thought of the vision I'd just experienced: of the golden-white glow and the love and beauty of the angels. I knew that I was completely and absolutely protected, blessed and guided. "By the grace of God," I thought. The angels saved me!

HELP FROM HEAVEN
by Candace LaPointe

I must share with you an experience that happened to me on October 1, 1997, which concerns Sister Mary Frances. While driving into work on a Monday morning, the traffic into Montreal was extremely heavy, bumper to bumper for miles, with people dangerously cutting one another off and tempers flaring. The approach to the Louis Lafontaine Tunnel is especially hazardous because trucks are restricted to the center lane. So not only do you have cars zipping in and out of the lanes, but some frighteningly big semi-trailers are also cutting in to get to the middle lane of traffic. My exit is immediately outside the tunnel off the right lane. While going through the tunnel, I always pray the rosary through the morning rush hour, but this morning I felt the need to add a guardian angel prayer.

As my car approached the tunnel, I couldn't help but notice a big white Cadillac patiently sitting on the right side of the highway. When I passed by, it miraculously nosed in behind me and in front of a gigantic tractor trailer, whose driver was not at all happy as he slammed on the brakes and downshifted to keep from hitting the Cadillac. I curiously checked the rear-view mirror to see what maniac was driving!

To my surprise and utter amazement the woman driver looked exactly like Sister Mary Francis, but perhaps a younger version, and as I looked back at her, she smiled the most beautiful, angelic smile! I laughed to myself because I had not thought of Sister Mary Frances in a long time and could not even imagine her driving a white Cadillac! Suddenly as I looked forward again, horror swept through me. The traffic had suddenly come to a complete stop in the tunnel. I slammed on my brakes and looked into the rear-view mirror and saw the huge semi-trailer, which hadn't changed lanes, speedily approaching the white Cadillac. Sister Mary Frances' look-a-like was doomed. I braced myself for a terrible crash. The sound of tires screeching was deafening but I felt no impact. Then I quickly checked the rear-view mirror and found the gigantic trailer truck sitting a millimeter behind my car. The Cadillac had vanished! It was not behind, beside, or ahead of my car. With all the traffic packed into the tunnel, it would have been impossible for it to have driven away. The space the Cadillac had taken was just the right amount to allow the truck driver to brake and avoid crushing my car to bits. All day long I thanked the Lord for sending His "Cadillac angel" to save my life.

Only later when I attended our prayer ministry session did I learn that Sister Mary Frances had passed away only a few days earlier.

A VISIT FROM MY GUARDIAN ANGEL
by Grace Thunder Frier

One day in February, 1990, I had an arthroscopic operation on my knee. It was performed in the surgeon's office without any pain killers.

After the surgery, I realized I could not drive my car home. The car was parked in the bottom lot of a hillside parking lot. That day the usual shuttle bus was not running to take me up the hill to the hospital where I could rest in the lounge beside a large pool of tropical fish. It would help to relax until I could call to get some help.

At first I looked up at the hill, impossible for me to navigate alone, and with a loud voice out of control, I said, "God help me," which resounded on the landscape. Immediately I heard a car start its motor and head towards me on the hillside road. The driver was an attractive young woman about thirty years old. She exclaimed, as she drove up alongside of me, "I am here to help you."

I thanked her and asked for a lift to the hospital entrance. She said after she left me off, "I will return later and take you to your car."

"Thank you very much, but I do not want to impose on your kindness. It must be close to your lunch hour."

There was no response. Then it really seemed clear that while she looked like an efficient young business woman, her business was not of this world. I was amazed how efficiently and quickly she navigated through the traffic to the hospital entrance.

After one or two hours of relaxing, I felt able to negotiate the downside of the hill. As I stood contemplating the possibilities of walking, all of a sudden the same little car arrived right in front of me, and the young lady exclaimed in her business-like voice, "I am here to help you."

Humbly with great gratitude I accepted the ride back to my car. Her manner and her serious attitude convinced me that she very definitely was my guardian angel. I was speechless and grateful beyond words as she disappeared up the hill.

After sitting for a few minutes, holding the wheel of my car, I started homeward on a cloud of unbelievable gratitude. The minute I could get to my phone, I called my daughter in Anacortes, Washington, and related the day's events. She was elated too, and said, "Mother, you have seen your guardian angel!" I replied, "There was never any doubt that "Augustine," (the name I gave my angel), was sent to help me and answer my prayer for help."

GUARDIAN ANGEL
by Wayne Hackett

Dear little child,
I am God's gift to you,
How great God's love for us,
That this should come to be.
The good God sent me here
To guide you night and day,
Protect you from all harm,
To find you if you stray.
To lift you when you fall
And dry away each tear.
To hear you when you call:
For I am always near.
To hold you in my arms,
When night time ends the day,
Protect from all alarms,

To listen as you pray.
And when, at last, you sleep.
You never have to fear:
For though the dark be deep,
Your Angel's always near.

CONCLUSION

We have traveled through just a few examples of the reality of our powerful angels and their interactions with us human beings. We have seen more of God's wonderful response to prayer in scripture, in the lives of the saints, and in our own lives. Our actual experiences with God's powerful and true friends, our beloved angels, fill us with awe and gratitude to God. All of which increases our faith.

All public revelation was completed and terminated with the death of the last scripture writer, Saint John the Evangelist.

However, the Catechism of the Catholic Church, in paragraphs #66b and #67 states, "Yet even if Revelation is already complete, it has not been made completely explicit: it remains for Christian faith gradually to grasp its full significance over the course of the centuries."

Throughout the ages there have been so-called private revelations, some of which have been recognized by the authority of the Church. They do not belong to the deposit of faith. It is not their role to improve or complete Christ's definitive Revelation, but to help live more fully by it in a certain period of history. Guided by the magisterium of the Church, the 'sensus fidelium,' knows how to discern and welcome in these revelations whatever constitutes an authentic call of Christ or his saints to the Church."

Our true friends, angels and saints sent by God, bring the good news of hope, of Christ's ultimate victory. We can say, "Yes or no," to God's perfect plan for our lives. God and his friends never will force us.

God's messages of love and encouragement surround and follow us through the ups and downs of daily living to keep our minds from becoming distracted by the rush, rush of worldly circumstances and attractions, for our restless hearts can be so easily closed up to his call of hope.

We are invited to recall in our own lives the events, the God-moments, the enlightenments that God sends along our path, and see in those incidents the windows through which we pilgrims can see God's ways, his wonderful promises, his love and providential care.

May our ever-faithful friends, our beloved angel-protectors, ever be the recipients of our gratitude and thanks all the way to heaven where we and our angels will be praising and enjoying God and one another forever.

Compilers Note:

The stories compiled in this book are printed with the express written permission of those who authored them. Letters are on file with A. M. Griffith.

ABOUT THE AUTHOR

Sister A.M. Griffith, while at Western Washington University in Bellingham, Washington, entered religious life in 1949.

She received a B.A. from Seattle University and has a Washington State Standard General Education Certificate. She graduated with a M.A. in Theology from St. Mary's College and did post graduate work at Marquette and Notre Dame Universities.

After teaching about fifteen years, she was very active in various religious education programs on the west coast, as well as doing catechetical missionary work in Alaska.

Sister A. M. Griffith lives in Anacortes, Washington, and for the last 24 years has been involved in training prayer teams via video tapes and personal visits. At the moment, besides writing this book, she still travels to her teams to give retreats and days of recollection and is at home for people who come for the Lord's healing and prayer.